JUST
A MOMENT
150 Opportunities
To Find Encouragement

GW00726120

Philip J S

MALKOSH PRESS

Copyright © November 2022 Philip J Seifert
ISBN: 978-1-7392018-0-7

First published in the United Kingdom in 2022 by Malkosh Press.
Printed in the United Kingdom by Book Vault, Peterborough.
Front cover original photo by 'Sergey Nivens' (Getty Images).
Cover photo accessed and edited with wording using Canva Pro.
Back cover design by Dynamik_design1 (Fiverr.com).

Orders for this book can be placed through the following website:
www.malkoshpress.co.uk
Contact with the author can be made through the following email
address: info@malkoshpress.co.uk

In accordance with the Legal Deposit Libraries Act 2003, a print
copy of this book has been sent to the British Library.

All Scripture quotations are taken from the King James Easy
Reading Study Bible, KJVER®. ©2001, 2007, 2010 by Kings
Word Press. Used by permission. All rights reserved. Unless
otherwise indicated, all Scripture quotations are taken from the
King James Easy Reading Study Bible, KJVER®. ©2001, 2007,
2010 by Kings Word Press. Used by permission. All rights
reserved.

All rights reserved. No part of this publication may be reproduced,
stored in or introduced into a retrieval system, or transmitted, in
any form, or by any means (electrical, mechanical, photocopying,
recording or otherwise) without the prior written permission of the
publisher (except in the case of brief quotations embodied in
critical reviews and certain other noncommercial uses permitted
by copyright law).

Every effort has been made to trace copyright holders and to
obtain their permission for the use of copyright material. The
Publisher apologises if there have been any errors or omissions
and would be grateful if notified of any corrections that should be
incorporated, which will be implemented at the first opportunity
in any future copies.

Dedication

I wish to dedicate this, my first book, to my late father, John, who went Home to be with the Lord on 28th May 2011, and also to my late mother, Lorna, who went Home to be with the Lord on 11th April 2022. They were everything my sister Lynne and I could ever have asked for as parents, and taught us about the Lord from our earliest days. Life was difficult for them, but their love for each other increased over the years and never diminished, despite many hardships.

'The memory of the just is blessed.'
Proverbs 10:7

Acknowledgements

I want to thank my wife, Di and my children for all their support during the compilation of this book. There were many late nights, and I want to express my appreciation to them for their patience. They are my greatest supporters, always cheering me on.

Thank you to my sister, Lynne, for the many hours she spent in proof-reading the script. Thanks so much for the advice and the changes which you brought to my attention. I definitely could not have got this far without that help.

Thank you to my congregation at Donaghcloney Elim Church for your kindness and for your prayers and support, which are so much appreciated.

Most importantly, thank You to the Lord Jesus Christ and for His patience with me, as He moulds and transforms and works in me. I pray that everything written here will go down to His praise and glory. For He alone is worthy.

Introduction

Daily life can be invaded by external forces which so quickly disturb our peace. It just takes that one moment, which seems to come from nowhere, to mess up our day or even our life.

In Ephesians 5:16, Paul exhorts us to '*redeem the time.*' The word there for *time* isn't necessarily the time on a clock or a watch, but is a different Greek word, '*kairos*', which refers more to a moment of opportunity. Redeeming the time really means to *seize the moment of opportunity*.

It is my hope that those who read this book over the next 150 days, God willing, would be able to seize a moment of opportunity. Those moments that invade your space with distress and frustration need to be countered with moments of strength and encouragement from God's Word.

There is no set time to read these devotionals. It could be first thing in the morning to set you up for the day ahead. It could be at break or lunch time, or it could be last thing before you go to bed, helping to filter out the things that have happened earlier and to align yourself with God's perspective on your day.

These devotionals are in no way intended to replace your own personal reading of God's Word, but are designed to be a supplement which helps to build up your faith. I trust you will have a mixture of moments where you will laugh, be encouraged, strengthened and, at the appropriate time, maybe even challenged.

This book came into being during moments of discouragement which invaded our world, just out of the blue. When we were plunged into a series of lockdowns in 2020, I felt that I wanted to encourage people going through the difficulties that had come our way, and decided to produce some devotionals on a Monday to Friday basis in video format via social media. Many pastors at this time found their 'job descriptions' evolving into that of video director, producer and editor! It was something that we certainly had never envisaged up until that period of time.

The videos began on Monday 23rd March 2020 and continued even when lockdowns had ended. The last devotional was broadcast on Friday 11th June 2021.

The devotionals began originally as, '*Just A Minute.*' They taught me a lot about how to reduce what I was saying into a shorter time frame, which can never be a bad thing for a congregation! But it became very difficult to keep to that one minute, and so I changed them to '*Just A Moment*' which gave me more scope to speak longer than sixty seconds! They then got a little longer, and morphed into '*Strength For Today*', with some of the congregation also taking part. The final format was '*The Two Minute Message*'.

It took a lot of time and discipline to put these messages together on a daily basis and also to record them, but it was something that I did enjoy. However, around June 2021, I felt that they had run their course. It was suggested that I should publish these messages, but I didn't really think much about it until recently. So finally, I have gathered some of those original messages and have created a number of new ones for this publication.

Most of the illustrations in this book are taken from everyday observations of life. I hope my family members don't mind me giving you too much of a glimpse into their lives! But I think it builds a bridge between author and reader.

I have heard many stories and illustrations over the years. It would be impossible to know the original source of them all. I have endeavoured to give credit where possible, but when I am not able to find the original source, I have used the phrase, '*Someone has said*' or '*You have probably heard it said.*' If there have been any copyright infringements, they are unintentional, and I would seek to rectify such a situation in future copies of this book.

The front cover of this book is representative of the difficulties that can come into our lives. In the background are dark clouds, which remind us of the clouds of discouragement and trouble that hover over us at times. The cracked ground at the bottom of the photo depicts the cracks and the brokenness that can tear us apart in our worst moments. But in the midst of the dark clouds and the cracked ground is an hour glass that is filled with light. An hour glass of course speaks of moments of time, and when we give our moments over to the Lord and rest in Him, a great light can shine in our hearts despite the darkness all around us.

As you set your moments aside to read these words, please remember that just a moment can absolutely change everything.

One moment, the prodigal was at his lowest point, ready to eat the pigs' food. In *just a moment* he had seen sense, repented and was on his feet heading home to his father's house. (Never give up on your prodigal).

Paul and Silas were locked up in prison, and suddenly, in *just a moment*, there was an earthquake. They were set free and the jailor and his household were saved.

Paul tells us that *in a moment*, in the twinkling of an eye, Jesus is coming again, and we shall be changed.

A lot can happen in *just a moment*. That's all it takes. Never give up. God is able to do more than we can ever ask or think – in His Own time-frame and in His Own way.

'*Just A Moment*' has not been published for any personal financial profit. Any profits which may be made from this book (after initial overheads and other expenses have been covered) will go towards our church building fund and church ministry in general.

My simple and heartfelt desire is that this little book may be a blessing and encouragement to many, and most of all that Jesus Christ would be glorified throughout its pages.

May God richly bless and strengthen you in the days ahead.

Philip J. Seifert

November 2022

DAY 1

Don't Look Back

Brethren, I count not myself to have apprehended:
but this one thing I do, forgetting those things which are behind,
and reaching forth to those things which are before....
Philippians 3:13

Roger Bannister set a world record in 1954 when he became the first man in history to run a mile in less than four minutes. His record was short-lived as John Landy beat it two months later. The two then met on 7th August 1954 in a historic race. As they came to the last lap, it seemed Landy would win. For some reason, he looked back over his left shoulder to try and detect Bannister. However, his opponent was on his right-hand-side and, as Landy's head was turned, Bannister crossed the line in first place. Landy lamented later that if he hadn't looked back, he would have won.

I wonder, as you look back at the last year of your life, how would you describe it? Whatever it has been like, there have no doubt been times when your faith has been tested, or when you have had disappointments, or when you have even made mistakes. While we can learn lessons from times of testing or from mistakes, yet it is not healthy to continually look over our shoulder at the past. God is the God of new beginnings. New starts are interwoven into nature itself, as the sun comes up every day and greets us with an opportunity for a fresh start. Lamentations 3:23 reminds us that God's mercies are new every morning.

Don't be distracted by the mistakes of the past. If anything needs forgiven, receive the cleansing of the Blood of Jesus, and move forward in the power of the Holy Spirit.

Your destination in this race is not behind you, it's ahead of you. Don't run in reverse. Your destination is to cross the finishing line as a winner. Keep your eyes on Jesus, and He will give you the victory.

DAY 2

Don't Quit

I press toward the mark for the prize of the
high calling of God in Christ Jesus.
Philippians 3:14

Yesterday we saw the importance of not continually looking over our shoulders at the past. Today, we continue the theme of running a race with the encouragement to keep on going, and not to quit.

In 2004, Paula Radcliffe was a favourite to win Olympic Gold in the marathon event in Athens. She had reached 23 miles of her target of 26 when, all of a sudden, she stopped. She looked back down the road and tried to get started again but, a few yards later, she couldn't go any farther, and her chances of gold had gone. Supporters were distressed as they saw Paula sit down on a kerb and sob. She didn't want to, but she had to quit. Her race was over.

Maybe in the last year, like Paula, only in a spiritual sense, you have had to pull over to the side, weary and exhausted with what life has thrown at you. In fact, at times, you have felt like quitting. What you need to know more than anything else, is that you are not alone. Help is available.

In the 1992 Barcelona Olympics, gold medal hopeful Derek Redmond was in the 400 metres semi-final. He started well, but suddenly his hamstring gave way, and he fell to the ground in pain. Determined to finish the race, he hobbled towards the finishing line. In one of the most dramatic moments of Olympic history, his father, Jim, broke through security, ran onto the track and Derek finished the race, leaning on his dad's shoulder, as a father helped his son over the line. Thousands in the crowd cheered, moved by this beautiful moment.

Isaiah 63:9 says that the Lord lifted His people up in their distress and *carried them* all through the years. He will *carry you* over the finishing line with His strength and power. Please don't quit.

DAY 3

Be There

*And the LORD said to Moses, Come up to Me into the mount,
and be there: and I will give you tables of stone, and a law,
and commandments which I have written; that you may teach them.*
Exodus 24:12

An anonymous person who bought a lottery ticket on 2nd October 2020 in a Belfast store was invited by the organizers to come forward by 31st March 2021 to claim their prize of £1 million. All they had to do was turn up. All they had to do was to *be there* with the ticket, but it didn't happen. They missed out.

In today's verse, Moses is also given an invitation to turn up, and to *be there*. God says, 'Come up to Me into the mount, and be there.'

That phrase, '*Be there*', means more than just turning up. It means to remain there for a while. It was going to be an intimate time with God, when His glory cloud would fill the mountain. And Moses just had to be there.

If Moses hadn't turned up, he would have missed out on the glory of God and the revelation which he received of the Law.

We, as God's people, have an invitation from God to be there in His Presence, and to have intimate experiences with Himself. In Psalm 27:8, God invited the Psalmist to seek His Face. It was an invitation to be there. The Psalmist responded, 'Your face, LORD, will I seek.' He turned up.

God wants to have intimate moments with you today. Don't miss out on special moments with God, and insights into His Word, by not responding to His invitation to come up the mountain and simply *be there*. Remain there. Stay a while in His Presence.

The rewards for doing so far surpass any lottery ticket winnings!

DAY 4

Start Asking Again

You lust, and have not: you kill, and desire to have, and cannot obtain:
you fight and war, yet you have not, because you ask not.
James 4:2

One day I bought a barbeque rib sandwich (with a lovely barbeque sauce) and I put the plate into the microwave. After a few moments I looked, and the rib sandwich was still sitting unopened in its packaging. I had put an empty plate into the microwave!

My mind later strangely went to James 4:2: 'You have not, because you ask not.' Just as I didn't get hot food *out* of the microwave because I didn't put any food *into* the microwave, so James is saying, that we do not receive some things from God because we do not ask. We don't put any request *in*, so we don't get anything *out*. We don't receive.

Now, while God *does* give us things which we never even thought of praying about, yet, generally, He has ordained that He works in answer to His people's prayers. Why then do we not ask for some things in prayer?

Maybe we feel God will say *no*. Well, as long as it isn't something wrong that you are asking for, you won't know the answer until you ask. Or perhaps you feel the thing you are asking for is impossible, but remember that God specialises in the impossible. Just ask and let Him decide. Then there are those who prayed for things years ago and have given up. If God has given you a definite *no*, then of course leave it. But if He hasn't, then can I encourage you to take up those prayers once again?

Start praying again for that vision God put on your heart years ago. Start praying again for that prodigal that you've given up on. Start praying again for that sick person you know whose situation hasn't changed for years. Kick-start those prayers again today. You can't expect to get anything *out* until you first of all put something *in*!

DAY 5

Telephone To Glory

Call to Me, and I will answer you, and show you
great and mighty things, which you know not.
Jeremiah 33:3

I had to make a phone call, and was met with the usual, 'All our lines are busy, you are third in the queue.' Imagine my surprise when, a few moments later, the message came back saying, 'You are now *fourth* in the queue!' That is the first time ever that an answering machine has moved me *down* the queue instead of *up*! It must have been a technical hitch.

When it comes to God's people calling on His Name, there are no answering machines, no being shoved to the back of the queue and no technical hitches (at least from Heaven's side). God is easily accessed by just a simple prayer, and the mention of His Name.

In 1963, President John F. Kennedy became the first President in history to have a direct hotline to the Kremlin in Russia, but we as believers have a greater hotline, to Jesus, to the One Who sits at the right hand of the throne of God. What a privilege. Someone has said that God's phone number is *Jeremiah 333* (33 verse 3). 'Call to Me, and I will answer you, and show you great and mighty things, which you know not.'

Yesterday, we saw that we lose out when we don't pray. 'You have not, because you ask not.' Today's verse encourages us with the wonderful possibilities that can happen when we dare to pray. When we call upon God, it is as if we unlock something, and we set something in motion. We don't know when or how it will happen, but God promises He will show us mighty things.

Don't forget to pray today. Who knows what great and mighty things God is going to do and show you in the days to come?

DAY 6

The Standing Lamb

And I beheld, and, lo, in the midst of the throne and of the four beasts,
and in the midst of the elders, stood a Lamb as it had been slain,
having seven horns and seven eyes, which are the
seven Spirits of God sent forth into all the earth.
Revelation 5:6

My wife, Di (pronounced 'G') comes from Brazil. Her Grandmother kept hens in the yard, and if family came round for dinner, it wouldn't have been unusual for her to take one of the hens and use it for lunch. One minute the pet hen would be running around in freedom, and the next minute it was Sunday roast. The hen that was killed never got up again. That is quite an obvious statement. When we think of the millions of animals that were sacrificed under the Law, not one out of all those animals that were sacrificed ever got up again and ran around. I think you know where I am going with this.

When we look at Revelation 5:6, we read about a Lamb as it had been *slain*. (By the way, that indicates that the wounds were still visible in some way. Someone has said that the only thing in Heaven which will be man-made is the print of the nails in Jesus' hands). But the unusual thing we read is that this slain Lamb is standing: 'S*tood* a Lamb as it had been slain.' That speaks of the glorious resurrection of Jesus Christ. *He was the only sacrifice in history that ever stood up again after being slain.* This scene of a standing Lamb is the Christian's guarantee that our future is secure. Jesus has overcome death, hell and the grave, and His victory means our victory. Because He lives, we shall live also, and because He lives, we can face tomorrow.

In this verse there is a *slain Lamb*, a *standing Lamb*, but look finally at the *situated Lamb*. Where is He? In the midst of the throne and the elders. Jesus should always have the central place wherever He is. He deserves the praise, the honour and the glory. Does the Lamb have the central place in my life today?

DAY 7

A Double Helping

You will keep him in perfect peace, whose mind is stayed on You:
because he trusts in You.
Isaiah 26:3

You see it as a name on houses; you see it on plaques on people's walls. The word *Shalom*. The Shalom peace that the Bible speaks of is a holistic peace. It's a peace that encompasses not just the mind, but also the soul, the heart, the body, the whole being. In the original Hebrew, the verse doesn't literally say that God will 'Keep him in perfect peace,' but it says, 'You will keep him in *Shalom, Shalom.*' The best way the translators could translate that was to say '*perfect peace.*'

When we used to go to the seaside as kids, there was a shop on the way that sold ice cream and it had something that I don't think I have seen since: a double cone. We used to love to stop there and get a chocolate scoop on one, and a strawberry scoop on the other. It was a double helping of ice cream.

Shalom, Shalom could be seen as a double helping of peace. A double anointing of peace. A supernatural peace that flows over the body, mind, soul and spirit. It is a peace that only God can give (not as the world gives), and a peace that the world cannot take away. It is only the child of God who can have this real peace, through sins forgiven by our Saviour, Jesus Christ.

This peace comes from the inside out, and not the outside in. Someone has said that the peace of God is not the *absence* of trouble, but the *Presence* of God. The world can be falling around you, and yet you can still experience this deep abiding peace in your heart. The key to enjoying this peace is when our minds are '*stayed*' or focused on God. Maybe recently we have lost some of that peace. Can I encourage you (as Helen H. Lemmel wrote) to 'Turn your eyes upon Jesus'? You know the rest of the song. Why not sing it now and meditate on Him?

DAY 8

Faith Without Clarity

By faith Abraham, when he was called to go out into a place
which he should after receive for an inheritance, obeyed;
and he went out, not knowing where he went.
Hebrews 11:8

We all like to know where we are going. When Di and I were in Paris for our honeymoon, we visited the Eiffel Tower. When we reached the general location via the Paris Metro, we emerged from the underground, and immediately in front of us were tall buildings. Being directly beneath them, we couldn't see past them, and so we couldn't see where the Tower was. We walked a little further, and then stopped a man who was walking a dog. I asked (in my worst French accent), '*Où est la tour Eiffel?*' He looked strangely at us, and for a moment, it seemed even the dog looked strangely at us. The man turned his head and pointed behind where we were standing. The tall buildings had now disappeared, and there was the Eiffel Tower in all her glory. We felt a little foolish!

Not knowing where we are going makes us uneasy. We like confirmation. We like clarity. When I read this verse about Abraham being called to go to a place of inheritance (but he didn't know where he was going), I often wonder what the conversation would have been like between Abraham and Sarah. '*OK, Sarah, let's pack our bags. We are moving.*' '*Where to?*' '*I haven't a clue. God just said to leave home and get moving.*' Can you imagine *the look* your spouse would give you if you came home from work with that news? Abraham didn't have any clarity at all when God told him to leave Ur and travel to who knows where? More clarity would come along the way, but he was just called to obey God with the little information that he had. God's will is very rarely laid out for us in a detailed step by step plan. Many times, it involves just obeying what He has told us for now, and to keep on trusting Him. In His time, He will let us know a little more. Faith believes what it cannot see and goes where it does not know.

DAY 9

Kingdom Influencers

And lead us not into temptation, but deliver us from evil:
For Yours is the kingdom, and the power, and the glory, for ever. Amen.
Matthew 6:13

Before I was married (yes, I remember that far back!), I was able to go almost wherever I liked, and when I liked; watch the football whenever I wanted, eat whatever food I wanted, plan the things that I wanted, go on holidays whenever I wanted. But then one day that all changed. Oh boy, how it changed! I had to readjust my thinking to family life. Instead of thinking as a single person, I now have to do what's best for my family. I cannot make decisions without taking my family into consideration, and that, of course, is only right.

When we are transformed from being unsaved to saved, then we also have to readjust our thinking. We no longer think like unsaved people. We no longer live for self and for our own little kingdom, but we live for His Kingdom. When it comes also to prayer, the Lord is trying to shape and mould our prayers into this kind of thinking, where we pray not specifically for what *we* want but for what *the Lord* wants in our lives, and for His Kingdom.

There are two types of people in this world: earth-dwellers and Kingdom influencers. Kingdom influencers are like Abraham, who looked for a city whose builder and maker was God. They are those who are in this world but not of it; those who live to be influencers for the Kingdom of God, rather than this world.

We may be saved today, but are we still living like an earth dweller? Are we like a married person who is living as though they are still single? Or are we living as the bride of Christ? Are we Kingdom influencers, who have a passion and desire to advance the Kingdom of our God? 'For Yours is the Kingdom, and the power, and the glory, forever. Amen.'

DAY 10

Out With The Old, In With The New

Behold, I will do a new thing; now it shall spring forth;
shall you not know it? I will even make
a way in the wilderness, and rivers in the desert.
Isaiah 43:19

God is always doing new things, in people's lives, in churches, in communities, in nations. He is a creative God. When you look at creation all around you and see the beauty of it, what makes you think He isn't creating beautiful and wonderful and amazing things in people's lives today? God is a God of freshness and newness.

Remember way back, when they didn't have sell-by dates on food, and you would get a loaf of bread and next day it would be stale? I remember as a boy we regularly got packets of crisps that must have been months out of date. They were horrible, by the way.

Did you know it's possible for our relationship with the Lord to get stale if we haven't received anything fresh? When was the last time we remember getting the Bible out and it was like a 'light bulb' moment, when the Holy Spirit showed us something fresh from His Word? When did we last spend time in prayer, not just to ask things of God, but to linger in His Presence and wait upon Him, and receive something fresh from Him?

We cannot live on past experiences. We dare not let things go stale between ourselves and God. Every now and again we clear out our cupboards of anything that is out of date, and similarly, we need to take stock of that which is old and stale in our lives and just clear it out. God doesn't want us to continue in the staleness of yesterday, He wants to do a new thing. He wants to blow a fresh wind of the Spirit over us to transform and refresh us from within.

God has so much more for you: an unending supply of new things and fresh things for you that He wants to bless you with. Out with the old, in with the new.

DAY 11

Paid In Full

And you shall let nothing of it remain until the morning;
and that which remains of it until the morning you shall burn with fire.
Exodus 12:10

Who likes roast lamb? Not everyone. However, they say a three-ounce serving has only 175 calories and half of your daily protein needs. I like lamb now and again, but just don't pass me the mint sauce! What's all that about? Mint on meat? Having said that, I do enjoy a certain Brazilian dish with the strange mix of pork and oranges.

In Exodus 12, as the people are given instructions about the Passover Lamb, they are told that the lamb has to be roasted with fire, and nothing of it must remain until the morning. If anything did remain, it had to be burned with fire. In other words, the whole lamb had to be completely consumed with the fire. There must be nothing left over.

One of the pictures that fire gives in the Bible is of judgment. When Jesus died on the cross, He faced the fiery wrath and judgment of God which was due to us. He faced it fully and completely. Just as you couldn't say there was any bit of the lamb left over at Passover (as it had to be entirely consumed), so Jesus had to face the full judgment of the *'fire'* of God. Having faced it fully, no-one can say that sin wasn't completely answered for at Calvary.

Consequently, satan cannot come to you and say that Jesus didn't die for a particular sin that you have committed because Jesus faced the full *'fire'* of the judgment of God, and He atoned for it all. That is why He cried out, 'It Is Finished!'

If any person (or even satan himself) tries to fill you with guilt and attempts to convince you that a certain sin hasn't been forgiven, send them straight to Calvary. Every sin question has been answered at the cross. Jesus paid it all.

DAY 12

Living From the Inside Out

*There is nothing from outside a man, that entering into him
can defile him: but the things which come out of him,
those are they that defile the man.*
Mark 7:15

One day I went out to do a few messages and when I came home, Di heard me laughing. She asked what was so funny, and I showed her my rugby top. It was inside out. The badge and the stitchwork also looked strange, as the underside of each was showing. People in the shops and one particular owner of a bookshop (whom I knew) must have seen it. I suppose I shouldn't really tell you about this in case you think I'm daft, but blessed is he who can laugh at himself, for he shall have endless amusement.

In physical terms, we don't expect people to wear things inside out, but in spiritual terms that's actually the way we are meant to do things. We are meant to live from the inside out, rather than from the outside in. Jesus changes the inside of our heart, and we consequently live it out.

Religiosity always focuses on the outward. Jesus said that the Pharisees were like whitewashed tombs (Matthew 23:27). They looked so beautiful on the outside, but were full of the bones of the dead, and were unclean. Not a pretty picture.

Religiosity sings the songs in church ever so sweetly, prays the prayers ever so vocally, listens to the sermons ever so reverently, but experiences change in the heart ever so rarely. The frightening thing is that inside each of us is a little Pharisee just bursting to get out!

The good news is that there is a power within us as Christians, which is greater than the little Pharisee within us. When we allow the Holy Spirit to work in us, He can produce changes in our hearts that transform the outward things which we both do and speak.

DAY 13

Look Up

Set your affection on things above, not on things on the earth.
Colossians 3:2

One of the most disorientating ways to start the day is when you forget to set your alarm clock the night before. You wake up thinking, 'Where am I? What day is it? Please let this be Saturday. Oh no! It's Monday and I'm late for work!' It just messes with your head for the rest of the day, all because you didn't set your alarm clock.

Paul makes a very important statement about something that we should make due diligence to set every day. 'Set your affection on things above.' This is a setting that you need to be intentional about, and make sure you set it, or else your affections are more likely to go to default settings (the things of this earth). Immediately in this verse we are confronted with this daily conflict between the things above and the things on the earth, and it can be a difficult battle.

Our verse today is begging us to ask ourselves this question, *where do my affections lie?* The story is told of a young man who found some money as he walked along the street. From that day onwards, he always kept his head down in the hope of finding some more. Over the years, he accumulated hundreds of pins, buttons, elastic bands, and a few coins. But by constantly looking down, he missed out on the beauty of the world around him. Just as that money which he initially found won his affections and kept him looking downwards, so the things of this earth can win our affections and keep us from setting our affections on Jesus.

Where do our affections lie? If our affections have been won over by Jesus Christ, then our sights will be fixed above because in the previous verse (Colossians 3:1) Paul reminds us that is where Jesus sits at the right hand of God. Keep looking up!

DAY 14

Stand Yer Ground!

*Wherefore take to you the whole armour of God, that you may
be able to withstand in the evil day, and having done all, to stand.*
Ephesians 6:13

I was speaking to a lady who was working at a ticket office at the entrance to a beach. Right from the start of the conversation, this lady kept moving forward into my face and into my space. My immediate reaction was to move backwards, but as I kept moving backwards, she kept moving forwards. Body language experts will probably tell you she was trying to assert her authority over me. It came to the stage where I had to make a decision to stand my ground, no matter how unpleasant her being in my face was, or else I was going to spend the whole conversation walking backwards!

In a similar way, the world is like that with the Christian. It is not content with passing laws that are contrary to the Word of God, but it wants to get into our face, assert authority over us, conform us to their way of thinking, and silence us as to what the Word of God teaches. Sometimes our knee- jerk reaction to the world being in our face and in our space is to go backwards. It is uncomfortable, so we retreat. But we have got to learn (as I learned with that lady whom I encountered that day) to stand our ground no matter how unpleasant it is. Show the love of God but stand in the truth of God's Word.

Ephesians 6:13 emphasises the importance of making sure we have put on the whole armour of God in the evil day, but having done all that, then to simply stand. His full armour is enough to protect you. Soldiers of that day had spikes in their shoes that dug into the ground and helped them to stand firm. Dig your heels in and stand firm in the Word of God. Or as we say in Northern Ireland, '*Stand yer ground.*'

DAY 15

You Are Here!

To the saints and faithful brethren in Christ which are at Colosse:
Grace be to you, and peace, from God our Father
and the Lord Jesus Christ.
Colossians 1:2

We were in Portugal recently visiting Di's mum, and went to a large fun-park. It had a dolphin show, an artificial beach with artificial waves, 'pirates' doing acrobatics, an outdoor swimming pool, a bird show, and lots more. As we walked along a path, I was taking it all in, until I looked forwards to discover that the group I was following was not my family! I couldn't find them anywhere, and Di didn't have her phone. It was disorientating. I am geographically challenged! Having searched for a long time, I went to get an announcement made over the public address system, but just before I did that, they turned up. Not knowing where you are is an unpleasant experience.

It is so important to know exactly where we are spiritually. Paul is writing here to believers and, while they are living *at Colosse*, yet they are really *in Christ*. I'm sure you have seen maps in parks which have a big red '*X*' on them indicating, '*You are here.*' God's Word reminds us that, while we are physically in this world (in Donaghcloney, in Belfast, in New York, in Sao Paulo, in Beijing), yet, as believers, wherever we are, we are spiritually *in Christ*.

When we aren't sure where we are, or when we feel lost, we start to panic. In this world, as we look around us, it is easy to panic, as the situations of life seem to overtake us, and we feel disorientated. However, when we realise exactly where we are in this world (*in Christ),* then we remember that we are within the grip of the One Who is above all things and that we are safe in Him, whatever comes our way. Next time you feel a little lost, turn to this verse and remember that, while you are in a world that is spinning out of control, yet the 'map' says, '*You are here.*' You are *in Christ.* And that makes all the difference!

DAY 16

Who Is On Your List?

We give thanks to God and the Father of our Lord Jesus Christ,
praying always for you,
Colossians 1:3

Paul had a prayer list, and on that list were people that he probably hadn't met in his life. Paul had most likely never been to Colosse. But as soon as he hears of those who have been saved, he prays for them as if they were his closest buddies. You see salvation creates a bond between people like nothing else. Someone has said that your prayers can go to places that you will never be able to go yourself. Somewhere in a prison cell in China or North Korea, a Christian is being persecuted for his or her faith. You don't know them personally, but your prayers leave your heart, and go up to the throne of God. They travel across the world, and enter through prison bars, into a damp, dark lonely cell. The Christian in that cell suddenly feels a comfort and encouragement in their heart by the power of the Holy Spirit, and they find strength to endure. All because you prayed for them, despite not having even met them.

There's nothing like the family of God. We can make lasting friendships with people who are complete strangers because we have this bond in Christ. Who is on our prayer list? Do we just pray for ourselves and our immediate family? Does our list extend to those within our fellowship? Do we thank God for them, and pray always for them? But not only that, how far do our prayers go? Have we broadened our horizons by praying for those outside our fellowship? For missionaries who are labouring for God across the other side of the world? For congregations and fellowships that have been established with people that we will probably never meet or see until Heaven? What about the underground church? Do we pray for them?

What's our prayer list like? Your prayers can reach where your feet may never walk.

DAY 17

The Power Of His Presence

*After these things Jesus showed Himself again to the disciples
at the sea of Tiberias; and on this wise showed He Himself.*
John 21:1

It was after the events of Calvary and the Resurrection. Peter said, 'I go a-fishing,' but he didn't do any *'a-catching'*! If he wanted to eat some fish, he would have to go to Greasy Joe's chip shop down the road, and get a fish supper, because he wasn't getting any catches that night!

Now, it was early morning and the disciples are probably tired and discouraged. Jesus appeared on the shore and asked if they had any food. They replied that they hadn't, and Jesus said to throw the net on the right-hand-side and they would find some. It turned out they couldn't haul the net in because there were so many fish. What made the difference? The power of His Presence.

The same disciples (before Calvary) forsook Jesus and fled from His Presence as He was arrested. They were a bunch of frightened disciples. But after Jesus ascended to Heaven, they went into Jerusalem, Judea, Samaria, and all the ends of the earth with the gospel, unafraid, bold and courageous even unto death. What made the difference? Jesus had said to go into all the world and preach the gospel, and that He would be with them always (Matthew 28:19,20).

With the power of His Presence, you can do things that you could never do on your own; things that you would never even have dreamed that you could do. Maybe you have been a Christian for a few years, or maybe you are a bit 'longer in the tooth'. Look back at your life before you were saved, and then look at the places God has brought you, and the things He has done through you. You never would have imagined it. Give Him glory today, for that's the power of His Presence in you.

DAY 18

You Anoint My Head With Oil

You anoint my head with oil; my cup runs over.
Psalm 23:5

Psalm 23 is about the Shepherd and the sheep, and we know that sheep can get easily frightened. We've all heard the term, *sheep worrying.* It is possible that, if a dog causes enough distress to a sheep, it can take a heart attack and die.

We have all been there, haven't we? Circumstances have put us in this place of extreme worry. Worry over family, over finances, over health, until it almost drives us to distraction. Just like the dog that worries the sheep to the point where it almost takes a heart attack, worry can overcome us so much that it may even affect us physically. The chest tightens, the sweat comes on the hands, and we are just frozen with worry or panic.

Our verse today says that the Shepherd anoints our heads with oil. Where are we attacked emotionally? In the mind. But this picture of the Shepherd anointing our heads with oil is a picture of the comfort of the Holy Spirit.

Apparently, there is a type of fly called the nose fly, and they lay eggs that hatch worms, which make their way into the sheep's head, causing great irritation. Sometimes that irritation is so extreme that the sheep tries to bang its head on the nearest thing it can find to stop the aggravation. There are times when we feel we are being driven to distraction, to the point where we literally feel we could hit our heads off the wall. Have you ever been there? We need to remember our Shepherd wants to anoint our heads with oil (the oil of healing, the oil of the anointing of the Holy Spirit of God).

Do you feel you are in that place of distraction and aggravation today? Be sure to put aside time to get into the place of quietness with your Shepherd and allow Him to apply the anointing oil over your spirit and over your mind.

DAY 19

His Voice Makes The Difference

My sheep hear My voice, and I know them, and they follow Me:
John 10:27

It's funny that the Bible depicts us as sheep, because sheep are not the cleverest of animals at times! Do you ever remember when you wanted to do something which your friend was also doing, and your (Northern Ireland) parent said, 'Well, if Johnny wanted to stick his head in the fire, does that mean you have to do it to?' Apparently, sheep would! It is said that if a sheep jumps over a cliff, it is likely that the one behind will do it also. Sheep easily lose direction and wander from the fold. Isaiah 53:6 tells us, 'All we like sheep have gone astray.' It's in our very nature to wander and to lose direction. Our Shepherd, of course, knows this, and so He gives us guidance and direction. We will not wander if we follow Him closely and keep our eyes on Him.

I heard the story of a man who went to Israel and saw what he thought was a shepherd driving the sheep from behind. He had been told that shepherds in the Middle East lead from the front, rather than driving from behind, and so he asked the tour guide about this. He replied, 'Oh that's not a *shepherd*, that's a *butcher!*' The butcher drives from behind as he brings sheep to the slaughter, but the shepherd leads from the front as he leads them away from danger.

We are told that the Good Shepherd knows His sheep by name. What a thought. He died for you individually and knows you personally. Jesus not only knows His sheep by name, but they know His voice and they follow Him for direction.

I don't know, but maybe you, Christian, reading this, are feeling a bit lost and lacking direction in your life. When was the last time you heard the voice of the Shepherd? Christians should know His voice daily and follow Him. Determine to get away from all the hustle and bustle of life and make some time to listen for His voice. His voice will make all the difference to your situation.

DAY 20

Evacuation!

Then we which are alive and remain shall be caught up together with them in the clouds, to meet the Lord in the air: and so shall we ever be with the Lord. Wherefore comfort one another with these words.
1st Thessalonians 4:17,18

Granda Seifert was an amazing man with great artistic talents. (He also used to preach alongside his father, and my father, before dad took ill). Granda was born in Switzerland and was brought to Northern Ireland to live when he was very young. He went back to Switzerland to do National Service in the Swiss Army. When World War 2 broke out in 1939, he enlisted in the British Army. His exploits took him as far as Burma. Probably the moment that he would never forget was his evacuation from Dunkirk in 1940. It is said that Churchill only expected 20,000 to 30,000 evacuees, but the figure reached over 338,000, which he quite rightly described as a miracle. This was the greatest military evacuation in history.

However, there is going to be a greater evacuation and it will be the greatest of all time. It will be the moment when Jesus Christ Returns, and evacuates every single Christian 'soldier of the cross'. At Dunkirk, unfortunately not everyone was rescued, including some who were wounded. But Jesus will take every single person who has come to Him for salvation to be with Himself. No wonder Paul called this great event the '*blessed hope.*' Whatever our beliefs on end-times, let us unite in this: Jesus is coming back.

What a moment that will be. I always remember, as Dad was being buried, the speaker at the graveside, Norrie Emerson, pointed out the fact that while it took four men to lower Dad's body into the ground, it will take just One to raise his body out of it again. We which are alive and remain shall be caught up together with our loved ones who have died and meet them in the air. We need to talk about and preach the Return of Jesus a lot more. Firstly, it reminds the unsaved that they need to be ready for that moment when Jesus comes back. Secondly, Paul reminds us to comfort one another with these words. And that's what we are doing now!

DAY 21

How Do You Read Your Bible?

It is the Spirit that quickens; the flesh profits nothing:
the words that I speak to you, they are spirit, and they are life.
John 6:63

Unfortunately the Bible can become dull to us when we read it in the dryness of our natural spirit, and without asking for guidance from the Holy Spirit. Jesus said that His Words are Spirit and life. It is the Spirit that gives them life.

I was at a meeting and afterwards books were being sold. I picked up one of the books, and to be honest, when I opened it up, it may not have been a book that I would have read by choice. If it had been on a bookshelf, I probably would have set it back after quickly leafing through it; not because it was bad, but it just wouldn't be what I would normally buy. But do you know why I bought it? Because I heard the author tell me a bit about the book at the meeting, and he was a great communicator. He held my attention. He whetted my appetite and, when they told us there were books at the back, I went and bought one, because I saw that book through the eyes of the author. I saw his passion and heard what his heart was saying, and I was hooked.

If we read the Bible through our own eyes, it will probably be very dry. But if we hear what the Author (God) has to say and if we get fired up by the passion of the Author, and hear His heart and let Him enlighten us, then the Bible will be a completely different book. It will be like dynamite. Someone has said that the Bible is the only book where the author is always present when you read it.

Please don't get me wrong about what I am going to say next. It is important to be able to study the Bible in its original language, if we want to understand it better. All good scholars of the Bible will seek to do that. But Smith Wigglesworth lets us know that there is something even more important than that. He said, 'Some people read their Bibles in Hebrew, some in Greek. But I like to read mine in the Holy Ghost.' You see, the Spirit gives the Words life.

DAY 22

Keep Your Distance!

Flee also youthful lusts: but follow righteousness, faith, charity, peace,
with them that call on the Lord out of a pure heart.
2nd Timothy 2:22

I was driving the car one day and couldn't believe my eyes because a car was tailgating a lorry. All that lorry had to do was brake slightly for any reason, and there would have been a major crash. He (or she) didn't know much about keeping their distance. During Covid, we were told to keep our distance. The infamous two metre rule was something that we never would have even thought could happen in a pre-Covid world.

The Bible also talks about keeping our distance. 2nd Timothy 2:22 instructs us to flee youthful lusts. Those lusts could be lust for money, power, or another person. Keep your distance. Joseph did exactly that when Potiphar's wife tried to seduce him; he literally ran for his life.

Maybe there will be something in your life today, and you may be tempted to give in to it, whether jealousy, anger, lust, gossip or unforgiveness. Run for your life from it. Keep your distance!

However, I am so glad that there was One Who didn't keep His distance from us. When we were at a distance from God, Jesus came near to us. He didn't keep His distance from lepers, but He touched them, and made them whole. He made Himself friendly with the outcasts of society and went to a cross to bridge the distance between us and God, and to bring us near to Himself.

Maybe as a Christian, you have failed recently, and your guilt has put a distance between yourself and God in regard to prayer, and intimacy with Himself. Don't keep your distance. Hebrews 4:16 tells us to come boldly to the throne of grace, that we may obtain mercy, and find grace to help in time of need. James 4:8 tells us to draw near to God and He will draw near to us. Keep your distance from sin, but don't ever keep your distance from the Lord. He loves to have you close to Himself.

DAY 23

A Peace You Can Feel

And the peace of God, which passes all understanding,
shall keep your hearts and minds through Christ Jesus.
Philippians 4:7

If we have peace with God, then we can have peace in all the other areas of our lives. You cannot have the peace *of* God without first having peace *with* God. You see, the bottom line is this. If you have had your sins dealt with at the cross, then no matter how bad things get, and no matter what satan throws at you, nothing can take away the peace that comes supernaturally from God Himself. You can experience the peace of God that passes all understanding.

Paul says that it shall keep your hearts and minds through Christ Jesus. That word '*keep*' in the original language is really a military word, and it means that God's peace will '*guard*' the very door of your heart.

That is what caused Horatio Spafford to write, when he had lost four of his children in a sea tragedy, 'Though Satan should buffet, though trials shall come, let this blest assurance control, that Christ has regarded my helpless estate and has shed His Own Blood for my soul. *It is well with my soul.*' Even in the worst nightmare of his life, he still had the peace of God, and he could say, 'It is well with my soul.' That didn't mean he enjoyed the storm in his life, it didn't mean that he didn't miss his children and wasn't deeply grieved, but it did mean that he experienced the peace of God in the midst of the storm.

The peace of God is something you can feel. Some people think there is no feeling in Christianity, that it's all knowledge and theory. Although our faith relies primarily on what God has *said* rather than what we *feel*, yet there is still place for experiencing God. I believe God wants us to *feel* His peace enveloping us. Horatio Spafford experienced Philippians 4:7 and you can too. Why not sit in His Presence right now and feel His peace?

DAY 24

You Haven't Lost It!

Peace I leave with you, My peace I give to you: not as the world gives,
give I to you. Let not your heart be troubled, neither let it be afraid.
John 14:27

Did you ever collect the kids from school on a winter's day, and they come walking out with no jumper on? Just to look at them makes you feel cold yourself. And then they start to moan and complain, 'Daddy, I'm cold!' You say something like this to them, in a semi-sarcastic tone, 'Well I'm pretty sure I put a jumper on you when you went into school! Why did you take it off?'

As we continue for another day on the theme of peace, if your peace has been disturbed and you want it restored, what you need to realise is that, in essence, you haven't really *lost* your peace. Now stay with me on this for a moment. Jesus said, 'My peace I *leave* with you' and 'I *give* to you.' We already have been *given* it! God will not take that peace away. It is an eternal peace.

Jesus also says in this verse, 'Let not your heart be troubled, neither let it be afraid.' *'Let not'* are key words. *Let not* (or don't allow) your heart to be troubled. It's up to us. When we don't rest in the peace that Jesus has given to us already, then we are literally doing what the kids were doing when they took that jumper off. They exposed themselves to the cold, even though they had been given something to keep them from the cold! They weren't walking in that jumper!

And sometimes we don't walk in that peace that we already have been *given*. We allow ourselves to think thoughts that are contrary to what this verse is telling us. Please don't get me wrong. I'm not minimising the things that happen to us, but Jesus has *given* us a peace and left it with us. We can't lose it as such; we just need to try to walk in it and rest in it, and let it envelop our very being. Is there anything we need to change in our thinking today in order to align ourselves with the truth of this verse?

DAY 25

Peace On Earth?

These things I have spoken to you, that in Me you might have peace.
In the world you shall have tribulation: but be of good cheer;
I have overcome the world.
John 16:33

A Sunday school class was asked to draw a picture depicting something to do with the Christmas story. When the teacher came to wee Johnny, she had to look at his picture a couple of times. His drawing depicted angels in the sky. The people were running about picking up some round, green objects off the ground, and putting them in baskets. So, she finally asked what it was. Johnny said, 'That's the angels saying, "On earth, *peas*, good will towards men," and the people are picking up the *peas* and bringing them home!' Johnny had mixed up his words, but there seems to be some truth in what he said. It seems there are more *peas* on earth that there is *peace*. Where could you go in this world to find peace?

Jesus told us that because we are living in a sinful world, we *shall* (not *might* or *perhaps,* but *shall*) have tribulation. It's a 'cert'. Our lives will experience trouble and our world will be shaken in one way or another. There is not one verse in the Bible that promises followers of Jesus a trouble-free life. Troubles come to the Christian just as they come to the non-Christian. The difference though is that the believer has Someone to turn to in the middle of their troubles. The good news is that Jesus reminds us that He has overcome the world, and '*in Me*' you will have peace.

Earlier I asked, where could you go in this world to find peace? The Christmas carols speak of peace on earth, but where is it? Well, there actually are places all around the world where peace can be found. In the heart of Christians. Our hearts contain the peace *of* God, because we are at peace *with* God through Jesus. The old saying goes like this: 'No Jesus, no peace. Know Jesus, know peace.'

DAY 26

Selective Hearing

If any man have ears to hear, let him hear.
Mark 4:23

You shout at the top of your voice so loudly that it surely could be heard miles away, 'Kids, come down and get your dinner!' But ten minutes later when they still haven't come down, they say they didn't hear you. Yet at other times, you can be standing next to them and whisper, 'Would you like a new toy?' and they hear that with no problem. This (as you know) is called *selective hearing*!

God doesn't want casual or selective hearers, but rather people who will listen carefully, and who don't just let His Word wash over their head without understanding and grasping what He is saying.

When Jesus told parables, and when the disciples didn't understand things that He had said, they came and asked Him what He meant. But many others didn't. It all just went over their heads, and they didn't try to go deeper or try to understand what He was saying. Jesus said that while it seemed they heard, yet they did not really, and neither did they understand. They were like the people of Isaiah's day who were dull of hearing.

I think there can be a danger of us, as God's people, being dull of hearing. We hear, but we don't hear. When was the last time we studied the Word for ourselves? Not just a casual reading, but in-depth, and asking the Holy Spirit to help us understand what we are reading. Not rushing away but taking time.

When we are called upon to hear in the Bible, it is never an invitation to hear just for the sake of hearing, but there is a definite reason for hearing. God doesn't want us just to hear and let that be the end of it. What good is that? But over and over we see that we have to hear and *understand*, we have to hear and *believe,* we have to hear and *receive,* we have to hear and *do*. How's our hearing?

DAY 27

Faithful In Small Things

His lord said to him, Well done, good and faithful servant; you have been faithful over a few things, I will make you ruler over many things: enter you into the joy of your lord.
Matthew 25:23

Some time back, we used the click and collect service at one of our local supermarkets. I went to collect our groceries, and they had given us more of a particular item than we had ordered. It wasn't a big deal, but the guy who was serving me said to keep the items. If it had been a supervisor who had told me that, then I probably would have done so, but he was just helping out, and didn't really have any authority. It didn't feel right, so I thanked him but asked him to take them back. Although the supermarket giant wouldn't have missed a couple of pounds worth of goods out of its millions, yet if that scenario was replicated at least once in every store in the UK every day, then no doubt it would soon add up to a lot of money. The point I want to make is that he was not being a good steward of his employer's goods.

We are also called to be good stewards of what God has given to us. He has given us gifts, and we are to put them to good use in His service, and to represent Him well. Unlike the supermarket employee, we are not to be sloppy in our service for the Lord, but to seek to advance His kingdom, rather than cut corners.

In today's verse, those who have represented their master well are called good and faithful servants. Are you feeling under pressure because you look at others, and you feel you aren't as 'successful' as them in serving God? Don't feel that way. Jesus says *'faithful servant'* and not *'successful servant.'* We aren't called to be successful as such (although we still give of our best), but we are called to be faithful. The verse then continues to make commendation for being faithful in a few things, with the reward of being made ruler over many things. Don't despise the day of small things. You may think what you are doing for the Lord is insignificant, but He sees it, and great will be your reward.

DAY 28

A Bumper Harvest

Then says He to His disciples, The harvest truly is plenteous,
but the labourers are few;
Matthew 9:37

As Jesus looked around Him, He saw a problem. There was a great harvest to be gathered in, but not enough workers to do the job. At the time when Jesus lived, we can only estimate, but the world population was around 150-300 million. Today it is around 7.8 billion. There have never been as many people in the world as there are today. Jesus said in John 4 that the fields are white and ready to harvest and, if it was true then, how much more now? There is a bumper harvest today, the fields are ripe with 7.8 billion souls, many of whom are potentially ready to give their lives to Christ if only someone will tell them how.

The task if you look at it, seems far too great. Since 7.8 billion is a lot of people, how can the job ever get done? Added to that, Jesus said that while the harvest is great, yet the labourers are few. And what can we do from the small patch where we are placed? Well firstly, we can send help to missionaries abroad. But secondly, the place where you are now is a harvest field where you and your fellowship, and the fellowships around you, have the privilege and responsibility to do the work of God. It's all yours! You cannot evanglise 7.8 million, but you can evangelise the souls that you have been given care of in your own harvest field.

You probably know the story of the boy who was throwing some starfish back into the ocean. A man stopped him and said, 'There are thousands of starfish on this beach; you cannot possibly make a difference for them all.' The boy picked up another one, and threw it into the ocean and said, 'Well, I made a difference for that one!' We can't evanglise 7.8 billion people ourselves, but we *can* make a difference to each person, one by one, in the harvest field to which we are called. Jesus said the night is coming when we won't be able to work. Let's get involved in our harvest field now.

DAY 29

What Am I Going To Wear Today?

Put on therefore, as the elect of God, holy and beloved, bowels of
mercies, kindness, humbleness of mind, meekness, long-suffering;
Colossians 3:12

A conversation with your wife maybe has gone something like this: 'We have to leave soon. What are you doing?' 'I'm getting changed.' Half an hour later: 'We're going to be late. What's keeping you?' 'I haven't got anything to wear.' 'What do you mean you've nothing to wear? You have a whole wardrobe full of clothes!' Clothes play a big part in our lives. Unless you wear a uniform to work, one of the first things that will come into your head when you wake up in the morning (apart from 'Where am I? What day is it?') is 'What am I going to wear?'

Paul addresses what we should put on as believers every day. The phrase, *'put on'* literally means to *clothe yourself* in these things such as mercy, kindness, humility, meekness, and patience. Previously, in verse 9, Paul has said that you have already put off the 'old man' and therefore you should be wearing your new clothes. Imagine if you got up one morning and decided to put on clothes that you wore forty years ago. Maybe they are embarrassing. Tartan trousers from the 70s? Or maybe those clothes are worn out and threadbare. Perhaps they are too short or tight. Our old spiritual clothes don't fit us anymore either. They are embarrassing. Why do they not fit us anymore? Paul addresses the believers in verse 12 as 'The elect of God, holy and beloved.' We are God's chosen people and Paul is saying that we should live a life consistent with our new identity in Christ.

Of course, that doesn't mean we will be perfect. None of us are. But it should be our intention each day, as best we can (with the help of the Holy Spirit), to walk in the new clothes that we have been given as the elect of God. If we sin, then we can come for cleansing, and He graciously renews us, giving us the strength to 'keep on keeping on', and living for Him each day.

DAY 30

Remembering Incorrectly

We remember the fish, which we did eat in Egypt freely; the cucumbers, and the melons, and the leeks, and the onions, and the garlic:
Numbers 11:5

God's people were complaining about the manna that God had provided for them and were remembering things incorrectly. They remembered their time in Egypt along with the fish, cucumbers, melons, leeks, onions and garlic. The only thing I would want to remember from that list is the melons, and maybe the onions, but the rest I can leave! But look what they said. 'We remember the fish, which we did eat in Egypt,' and what's the next word? '*Freely.*' No, they did not eat it *freely*. They were in Egypt as slaves and lived under an awful burden. They had already forgotten that God had set them free from the bondage of Egypt. So what if they had to eat manna? Far better to eat manna in a desert for the rest of their lives in *freedom*, than the luscious food of Egypt as *slaves*. Their perspective was all wrong. How they remembered the past was all wrong.

It is possible sometimes for us as Christians to slip into this danger of remembering things incorrectly. No doubt satan has come at some stage to taunt or tempt most Christians, reminding us about the wicked who are prospering, who live to a good age, and have a big house, big cars, holidays, and are living in pleasure. He tells you that the Christian life is a difficult one, and you seemed to have it so much easier before you were saved.

Jesus said that His yoke is easy and His burden is light (Matthew 11:30). Compare that to what the Bible says about the unsaved. The way of the transgressor is hard (Proverbs 13:15). It says that the wicked are like the troubled sea that is constantly tossed up and down, and they have no rest (Isaiah 57:20). Don't look at your past through *rose-tinted* glasses. Look at them through *redeemed* glasses, and praise Jesus for setting you free!

DAY 31

A Two-Way Process

For this is the will of God, even your sanctification,
that you should abstain from fornication:
1st Thessalonians 4:3

God didn't just save you to save you. He saved you to sanctify you. To set you apart to Himself and make you holy.

One of the problems I think we have in evangelical circles is that we focus so much on getting people saved that, once they get saved, they think that's it. They have their ticket to Heaven and escape route from hell, and that's it. That of course is not '*it*'. Salvation is more than just a ticket to Heaven and an escape route from hell; it's a process of change and transformation that begins in the heart.

The verses in this chapter go on to say that we should know how to master (or control) our bodies. Paul says that the Gentiles who don't know God just do whatever they please. If it looks good, then they do it, regardless of morality or consequences. However, it is God's will for the Christian to be able to control their bodies and control their thoughts, all of course through the power of the Spirit.

But here is the thing. If it is God's will to sanctify us, and if God wants us to be in control of our bodies and minds etc., then it obviously should be *our will* also. Sanctification is a two-way process. While it is a work of God and we cannot sanctify ourselves, yet it does require our co-operation. Sometimes we say, '*I want the will of God for my life, but I don't know what it is.*' Well, while there are some things we may not know, yet there are some things that are very plain. It is God's will for every Christian, that we should be sanctified. If we can die to self and get on board with God's will in this area of our lives, who knows the amazing things that He will be able to do as we allow Him to mould us and shape us and sanctify us.

DAY 32

Jars Of Clay

But we have this treasure in earthen vessels,
that the excellency of the power may be of God, and not of us.
2nd Corinthians 4:7

This verse reminds us that we are earthen vessels (or jars of clay). In New Testament times, jars of clay were 'a dime a dozen'. They were cheap and had short life spans. When one broke, it wasn't a big deal, as they were easily replaced. They were of as little importance almost as today's fast-food containers.

Just like jars of clay, we too are easily broken. Paul goes on to describe in what ways we can be broken. He talks about being troubled on every side, perplexed, persecuted and cast down. It doesn't matter who it is, whether Christian or non-Christian, we are all jars of clay, and are all easily broken. Death, disease, troubles, problems, disasters are no respecter of person or religion. They come to us all.

But there *is* a difference between the Christian and the non-Christian. The Christian jar of clay, we are told here, contains a treasure, and that treasure is Jesus Christ and the power we receive through knowing Him. Because of this, Paul says, yes, we may be troubled on every side, but we aren't distressed. We may be perplexed but we aren't in despair. We may be persecuted, but we aren't forsaken. We may be cast down, but we aren't destroyed.

The Japanese specialise in Kintsugi art, which has the idea of taking something that is broken and restoring it. They would take a jar or pot that is broken and restore it using a special glue containing 24kt gold leaf. The gold shows where the cracks once were and makes it even more beautiful than it was before the damage was done. (Look up the charity, Kintsugi Hope, to find out more). We can give the scars and cracks of our lives to Jesus. And this treasure within our jars of clay can make something beautiful again out of our scars. Unlike the jars of clay which were 'a dime a dozen', we are of great value to God.

DAY 33

Sticks And Stones

Wherefore comfort yourselves together,
and edify one another, even as also you do.
1st Thessalonians 5:11

Elijah was sent into a spiral of discouragement by one of the smallest weapons in the world: the tongue. The man who had stood strong against 450 prophets of Baal is floored by words from one woman. One of the greatest sources of discouragement is the spoken word. Words can wound. Your day may be going really well when, all of a sudden, something is said that you weren't expecting, and it's all downhill from then onwards. Many a Christian has stood against the fiery darts and attacks of the devil, and stood strong, only to be floored by some words of discouragement, sometimes even from another Christian.

As children, we may have repeated the words, 'Sticks and stones may break my bones, but names will never harm me.' But that's not true, for they *do* hurt. If you want straight talking, go to the book of James. He says that the tongue is like a fire, it is a world of wickedness and is set on fire by hell. Yes, he's talking about that little piece of flesh in our mouths that can either break a person or make a person. He also says the tongue is poison.

Did you know it's easier to tame a lion than to tame the tongue? James says that every type of animal has been tamed by man, but no-one can tame the tongue. Isn't that amazing? The good news is that although *no man* can tame the tongue, yet if we yield it to the *Holy Spirit*, He can set the tongue on fire of Heaven!

Let's determine to be a Barnabas. In Acts 11, we are told about Barnabas who, of course, was a great encourager, but the way it is written in the Greek implies that he encouraged people over and over again. This was the sort of person he was. Let's encourage one another. Mark Twain is meant to have said, 'I can live two months on one good compliment.' And it's true. Somebody just needs to hear an encouraging word today.

DAY 34

Take It To The Lord

The righteous cry, and the Lord hears,
and delivers them out of all their troubles.
Psalm 34:17

The righteous cry. If you are saved, that is you. You may not feel righteous. You may actually feel a failure. But because you are in Christ, you are *positionally* before God declared righteous. God doesn't see your sin, but, instead, He sees the Righteousness of Jesus Who died for you. Surely we will never cease to be amazed by that incredible thought.

And so, this verse is about you. The righteous cry. When was the last time you cried to the Lord about the situation you are facing?

Hezekiah got a letter from an enemy that was threatening and mocking. *'Ha! Hezekiah! You have heard what the King of Assyria has done to other nations, and do you think you shall be delivered?'* And you can almost imagine the evil laugh of the villain behind the letter. *'Mua-hahahahaha'!*

Did Hezekiah show it to his advisors? No, he didn't. He also didn't head to the House of Commons, or the House of Lords, but to the House *of the Lord*. Where do you go when you are in trouble? The first port of call, before we go to any person, should be what Hezekiah did. Go straight to the Lord. We read Hezekiah spread that letter out before the Lord and cried to the Lord.

Do you know what happened? The angel of the Lord defeated the Assyrians and delivered Hezekiah and his people from the enemy.

Maybe you have received a letter that contains bad news; a medical report, a financial difficulty, or maybe a text message from someone who has hurt, annoyed, threatened, or lied about you. Spread it out before the Lord, pray over it, and cry out to Him. It's Biblical!

Bring your burden to the Lord and leave it completely with Him.

DAY 35

Returning Good For Evil

Not rendering evil for evil, or railing for railing:
but contrariwise blessing; knowing that you are thereunto called,
that you should inherit a blessing.
1st Peter 3:9

Someone has said, 'To reward good for good is *man-like*; to reward evil for evil *animal-like*; to reward evil for good is *devil-like*; to reward good for evil is *Christ-like*.'

The world notices when we, as Christians, reward good for evil, and when we love those who hate us. Many have been converted having observed the life of a Christian who has rewarded good for evil. It is possible as Paul observed Stephen and heard his words of forgiveness, that this experience was something which spoke to him later on.

In 1956, five missionaries left America to evangelise Auca Indians in Ecuador. Each of the five missionaries was brutally murdered by the tribe. In 1957, Elisabeth Elliott, one of the widows, authored a book called *Through Gates of Splendour,* and she wrote, 'The prayers of the widows themselves are for the Aucas.' Elisabeth Elliott, and a sister of one of the missionaries, Rachel Saint, went back and lived among the tribe, and soon there were conversions, including three of the tribesmen who had murdered the missionaries. It was only the love of God and the power of the Spirit of God that could show such love as this.

Humanly speaking, they had no reason to go back and they had no reason to forgive, but that's the power of Christ in a life, and it only can happen when we yield ourselves to Him. It could not have happened in this way if Elisabeth Elliot and Rachel Saint had decided not to love those who had killed their loved ones.

That same love will help you also to return good to someone who has meant evil for your life.

DAY 36

Consecration

And he laid it upon my mouth, and said, Lo, this has touched your lips; and your iniquity is taken away, and your sin purged.
Isaiah 6:7

Isaiah had said that he was a man of unclean lips. His lips weren't being used to their full potential. When the coal from the altar touched his lips, they were consecrated, and were used to speak the Words of God.

There are members of our bodies that are not being used to their full potential for God, just like Isaiah's lips. We need a touch of the fire of God from off the altar. When that happens, our feet will begin to go again to the places God wants us to go, our hands will do things for God that we haven't done for a while, and our lips will start to speak things again for God that we haven't been speaking. Our minds will be touched, and we will start thinking thoughts that God wants us to think, our hearts will be stirred, coming alive again with His compassion, and we will go out and reach the world around us with members of our bodies that have been resurrected to serve God once again.

Will we consecrate ourselves afresh to Him? Will we give over every member of our body to the Spirit of God to use as He pleases? During World War 2, the Government of the day could have requisitioned your house or your car to use for the war effort, whether you liked it or not. God calls us to *willingly* give over our hands, our feet, our mouths, in this war for the souls of men.

B.H. Clendennen once said, 'The only thing necessary to reach this world for God is people full of the Holy Ghost.'

When we put all of our lives on the altar (every part of our being, each member of our body), there is no telling what God can do through a soul that is sold out for Him.

DAY 37

The Spin Cycle Of Life

*Rest in the LORD, and wait patiently for Him: fret not yourself
because of him who prospers in his way,
because of the man who brings wicked devices to pass.*
Psalm 37:7

Rest is a place of peace, a place of quietness. There's no struggling, no activity, just rest. We all make sure that we get our physical rest, at least to some extent. But what about mental, spiritual and emotional rest? We tend to major on the physical and minor on these other aspects. So often our minds are agitated with things that are going on in our lives, and the whole scenario goes round and round in our minds, and there's no rest.

The joke is told about a boy who went into a shop to buy washing powder. The shopkeeper asked him what he wanted it for, and the boy replied that he was going to wash his hamster. The shopkeeper tried to tell the young lad that you don't wash hamsters in washing powder. The boy thought he knew better and went away with his purchase. The next day, the boy was back in the shop, looking sad. The shopkeeper tried to be sensitive about it, but he couldn't hold back any longer, and asked if it was the washing powder that killed his pet. The boy said, 'No, I think it was the endless spin cycle of the washing machine that did it!' Please note that no animals were physically harmed in this story, it is only a joke!

What *isn't* a joke, is that sometimes the spin cycle of everything that is going on in our minds can drive us to distraction and despair, and even begin to affect our faith. Many times, we just need to take a step back, and realise the spin cycle isn't doing us any good, and we just simply need to rest in God. Jesus says to the weary and heavy laden, 'Come to Me....and I will give you rest' (Matthew 11:28). Many times, we quote that verse to the unsaved, but it's for us too. Having come to Jesus for salvation, let us then experience that rest and peace which He won for us at Calvary.

DAY 38

The Restoration God

He restores my soul: He leads me in the paths
of righteousness for His name's sake.
Psalm 23:3

You may have seen a TV programme called *The Restoration Man,* and so I have called this message, *The Restoration God.* Our God is a master builder, but not only that, He is in the restoration business too. Aren't you glad He is? Where would we be if He was not?

Think of an old broken-down house just lying there. We see them now and again on our streets. Some houses and buildings have been boarded up for years and are overgrown with weeds. Most people would just let them lie there and rot. But one person out of thousands will look at that ruin and think, '*I can do something with that. I can see that building, not as it is now, in ruin and overgrown, but I see it as it can be when I get to work on it.*'

And that is like us. We were lying there in sin, just rotting away. In fact, the Bible says in Ephesians 2:1 that we were '*Dead in trespasses and sins.*' There was no reason why anyone would take any interest in us. But Jesus came along and looked at us, and He knew He could do something with us. He saw us, not just as we *were*, but He saw us how we *would be* when washed and cleansed by His precious Blood.

Just like the Good Samaritan did with the man who had been left for dead (others passing him by, thinking him worthless), so our Heavenly Good Samaritan stopped where we were, picked us up, and restored us, bringing us new life.

It is possible for someone to come and look at an old building with interest in it, but once the assessment comes back, they decide that there is too much work to be done. It is too far gone. There is no person that God cannot restore. There is no-one too far gone for Him to do His Master-Building. God is *The Restoration God.*

DAY 39

Out Of The Ashes

He has made everything beautiful in its time:
Ecclesiastes 3:11

On 6th August 1945, an American B-29 bomber dropped the first ever atomic bomb over the city of Hiroshima. It released more energy than all the rest of the World War 2 bombs combined. It wiped out 90% of the city, and killed anywhere from 100,000 to 150,000 people, with more to follow from the radiation. Some reported that it seemed the city had disappeared, with whole streets vapourising. Surely there could be nothing more horrifying and destructive than this?

However, somewhere along the line, the leaders of Hiroshima put a plan together. They had a vision to re-build, they had a plan to restore, and today Hiroshima is a beautiful city that has risen out of the ashes of destruction.

In a similar way, a massive 'bombshell' came over the human race the day that Adam sinned. What destruction it brought, not only to the world around us, but more importantly to the heart of man. Could mankind ever recover from this? Surely there was no way back from the utter destruction that sin had brought to the human race.

Just as the leaders of Hiroshima had a plan to rebuild, so, even from before the foundation of the world, God had a masterplan. He had a wonderful vision for mankind to raise us up again from the ashes of defeat and destruction. That plan was fulfilled at Calvary's cross, when Jesus defeated sin, hell, death and the devil. He made a way whereby we could be restored again.

Our lives at one time could have been represented by a pile of ashes. We were without any hope at all. But Ecclesiastes 3:11 tells us that He has made everything beautiful in its time. This is the God Who raises us again from the ashes.

DAY 40

Greater Than Before

So the LORD blessed the latter end of Job more than his beginning:
for he had fourteen thousand sheep, and six thousand camels,
and a thousand yoke of oxen, and a thousand she asses.
Job 42:12

The word *'restore'* can mean to repair, or return to a former condition. In the Bible we find that although these meanings are included in restoration, yet many times it can mean more than just restoring to its *former condition*. You see, we have a God Who is abounding in His grace and mercy, and Who restores above and beyond what was done in the past.

Look at Job's story. God blessed him at the end with more than he had at the beginning. James in chapter 5:11 takes us to the close of Job's story, and he says that the *end* of the Lord is mercy and compassion. We may be facing a trial, and we don't know whether we are at the start of it, or halfway through it, but know this: that the end result which the Lord is working out, is mercy and compassion. That is what you should expect of Him.

And as you ask God maybe even today for restoration, I want you to look by faith. I don't want you to think that God *might* just restore you by the skin of your teeth, but that He can restore you *more abundantly* than you can even ask or think.

It's time for God's people to stop restricting God. It's time for Christians to stop being paralysed by what they *think* God will or will not do, and it's time for us to reach out in faith and see the potential of what He is *able and willing* to do when we yield to Him. Have you ever looked back to the passion you had for Jesus when you were first saved, and thought, *'Oh Lord, restore me to what I was back then?'* With respect, please stop asking that. Rather ask God to restore you in a *greater* way, and with a *greater* filling of His Spirit than you have ever known in the past.

That's the kind of God we serve!

DAY 41

The 'Mastermind' Verse

*Being confident of this very thing, that He which has
begun a good work in you will perform it until the day of Jesus Christ:*
Philippians 1:6

When someone restores something, they take a real, personal interest in it. It's a labour of love. Maybe someone is restoring a car. They spend their spare time and money doing it. They just love working at it. They don't have to. Nobody has forced them to do it. They have seen the car in a terrible state and have had a vision of how it can be lovingly restored, and they work away at it.

I want to remind you that, as God restores us, it is a labour of love. He is keenly and intimately interested in you. In every little detail.

I call today's verse, *The Mastermind Verse*. There is a quiz show in the UK called *Mastermind*, and the host who was associated with it for many years, Magnus Magnusson, had a catchphrase. When he went to ask a question, but the buzzer sounded to indicate that the person was out of time, he would continue with the question, and say, *'I've started, so I'll finish.'* Philippians 1:6 reminds us that God has started a work in us, and He will finish it. Without the shadow of a doubt. Don't be discouraged, God is still working on you and in you.

God's restoration doesn't cut us off from future fruitfulness but gives us hope and a future. When David had sinned with Bathsheba, in his Psalm of penitence he asked God to restore the joy of his salvation, but then he added, in Psalm 51:13, 'Then will I teach transgressors Your ways; and sinners shall be converted to You.' He felt he had a future in God. He had confidence that God would restore him, and not only that, but use him once again for His glory.

There is hope in God. He will restore. He will refresh. He can use you once again for His glory. He hasn't finished with you yet.

DAY 42

Thirsting For God

For I will pour water upon him that is thirsty, and floods
upon the dry ground: I will pour My Spirit upon your seed,
and My blessing upon your offspring.
Isaiah 44:3

Are you thirsty for God? Are you crying out for Him? Are you desperate for Him today? I believe that it is when we are at our thirstiest for God (and because of that, at our lowest point of humility) He loves to pour out the blessing.

The publican beat his chest and said, 'God be merciful to me a sinner,' and he went to his house justified. Naaman, at first too proud, eventually did what God's prophet asked of him, and humbled himself, dipping in the dirty Jordan river seven times. On the six occasions that he dipped himself and came up, he still had leprosy. But as his faith pushed through that barrier, and he went down the seventh time in his deepest humility and desperation, he came up differently this time. God poured out the blessing on him.

In the story of the Greek Gentile woman who called out to Jesus for help for her daughter who was demon possessed, initially Jesus seemed to knock her back, but He was testing her. He said it wasn't right to take the children's bread and give to the dogs. (That was a term for Gentiles by the Jews. The Jews were the blessed children of Abraham, and the Gentiles were the dogs). How many of us would have walked away? But she cried out in her humility and desperation, 'Yet the dogs eat of the crumbs which fall from their master's table' (Matthew 15:27). She was thirsty for the blessing and received it.

Are you hungry and thirsty for God today? Are you in a place of humility, but also of desperation, seeking for more of God? Then keep a look out, for you can expect the showers of blessing to fall.

God loves to pour out water on those who are thirsty.

DAY 43

Building On The Rock

Therefore whosoever hears these sayings of Mine, and does them,
I will liken him to a wise man, which built his house upon a rock:
Matthew 7:24

In this story of the two men who built their houses, one upon the sand and one upon the rock, you will notice that the storm came to both houses. Sometimes we are inclined to think that because we are Christians, no storms should come our way. But we do not read of this incorrect theology anywhere in the Bible. The force of the storm was the same for both men. It was ferocious. The Christian doesn't necessarily get an easier storm than the non-Christian. They come with the same force on both.

What makes the difference then? The foundation upon which the house is built. Jesus says that the house that was built on the rock did not fall, for it was founded on a rock. You cannot be destroyed, you cannot be overcome, if you are standing on the solid Rock, Jesus Christ. As a pastor, I have sat with people who have had severe storms in their lives, people who have been told bad news, people who were facing uphill struggles, and even people who have been facing the valley of death, yet because they had built their foundation on the solid Rock, they had peace in their hearts. I often wonder how people face these things without Jesus.

Many years ago, a young boy was shipwrecked. He survived the whole night long, shivering and freezing, while holding onto a rock, until another boat came and rescued him. There was a press conference afterwards, and a journalist asked a silly question. 'Did you tremble when you were hanging onto the rock?' The young lad replied, 'Oh yes sir, I trembled alright, but the rock didn't!' At times, fear can overtake us as we go through the storms of life. We may at times tremble. But the Rock (Jesus) never trembles and never moves. He is more secure than the Rock of Gibraltar!

DAY 44

Building On Sand

And every one that hears these sayings of Mine, and does them not,
shall be likened to a foolish man, which built his house upon the sand:
Matthew 7:26

Have you ever done anything foolish or stupid? Like telling your passenger to turn down the car stereo so you can see better to drive, or tried to pour your coffee out the car window, only to discover it was closed? One time while driving up a one-way street, I was waiting in a queue until I realised it was a line of parked cars, all in a row!

We all do foolish things. But there's foolish, and then there's really foolish! Who on earth would build a house on the sand? But yet that's what Jesus compares someone to, who builds their life on something other than Himself. It's that foolish. And Jesus isn't mincing His Words here.

The foolishness of this situation is glaringly obvious to anyone. If I came and told some friends that I had bought part of a beach and was building a house on the actual sand (after they would initially laugh, and then realise that I wasn't joking), I would hope that they would plead with me to come to my senses, and not throw my money away. I would hope that they would love me enough to try and show me the big mistake that I was making.

Similarly, we have friends and loved ones, who are building spiritually on the sand. There is a world out there full of people whom we don't know, and they are doing the same. Just as I would hope that people would love me enough to tell me that I was doing something foolish, surely, we at the very least 'owe' it to our friends, loved ones and the world around us to pray for them, and look for opportunities to lovingly show them the precarious place that they are in, and tell them of Jesus, Who is the sure foundation on which to build. They are blinded to their foolishness by the god of this world, satan. We have the truth which can set them free.

DAY 45

Low Battery

But they that wait upon the LORD shall renew their strength;
they shall mount up with wings as eagles; they shall run,
and not be weary; and they shall walk, and not faint.
Isaiah 40:31

Our kids have electronic games that of course need charged. I'm amazed by how close an eye they keep on the battery levels. Some nights before going to bed, they ask me to charge their devices, as they are maybe around 5% or whatever. And boy, are they on my case if I forget! We had to laugh one day, while out walking. Ellie was tired, and she said, '*My battery is at 10%.*' She was measuring her strength as if it were a battery!

I wonder if I asked you, how would you measure your spiritual battery? Especially after the last couple of years of Covid, the Ukraine war, and an energy crisis! Add to that the ordinary stresses and strains of everyday living. Maybe you feel you are hovering around 10%, or even that your battery has run out. The thing to realise is that, no matter how great in the faith you may feel you are, we are all prone to spiritual weariness, and even burnout. Whether we are someone young like Mark, who deserted Paul and Barnabas, or whether we are a seasoned Elijah who hid in a cave, it can come to us all. There are no spiritual superstars. We are all human, and we rely on a higher power.

How do you get your low battery recharged? Isaiah 40 tells us that whether you are faint (that's low battery!), or even if you have no might (empty battery!), yet the Lord increases strength. How? By simply waiting on Him. That phrase means to look expectantly to Him. '*They that wait upon the Lord shall renew their strength.*' The word '*renew*' here really means to exchange your weakness for His strength. Isn't it amazing that when God exchanges with us, we always seem to get a great deal? We exchange our sins for His salvation, our spirit of heaviness for a garment of praise, and our weakness for His strength. What an amazing exchange!

DAY 46

Geese To The Rescue

And if one prevail against him, two shall withstand him;
and a threefold cord is not quickly broken.
Ecclesiastes 4:12

I always have a wee chuckle at a short poem my Granny McKinley loved to recite: '*To live above with saints in love, that will indeed be glory. To live below with saints you know, now that's a different story*!' One of the complexities of church life is getting along with different people who have different personalities and different ways of thinking. However, the Bible over and over points out how vital it is that despite our differences, we need to have unity.

I know very little about geese, but what I do know is to keep well away from them when we go for a walk in the park! Once they start squawking at you, and going for you, it's not the nicest of experiences. But those who do know about geese tell us that they fly in a V-formation, which helps them make greater progress than if they flew separately. The amazing thing I remember hearing was that when one of them is wounded, two others fly out of the formation, and follow it down to help protect it. Isn't that beautiful? That has changed my opinion of geese. Slightly! And that's what the church should be like. Wouldn't it be nice if someone from a church was sick that maybe two or more people, (not just the minister), would call round with the person who is sick, and just say, 'You're one of us, and we want you to know we are here for you.' Unity is relational. It's more than just *saying* we are united; it is *lived out*.

As the believers waited for the out-pouring of the Spirit in Acts 2, it says they were there with one accord. There is a difference between being together and being together with *one accord*. You could have a thousand people together in one building, but they might not all be together with one accord. Unity is our strength. The ancient saying rings true. 'United we stand, divided we fall.'

DAY 47

The Aroma Of Unity

Behold, how good and how pleasant it is for
brethren to dwell together in unity!
Psalm 133:1

David describes unity as good and pleasant. The Hebrew word for pleasant suggests a pleasing aroma. A favourite part of Christmas Eve for me is when there is a lovely aroma that fills the house as the turkey is cooking, and the smell always draws me into the kitchen to pick a piece of bacon off the top of the turkey and eat it. I also love the smell of a particular fast-food chain, and it draws me to the drive-in take-away! Many people love the smell of freshly baked bread, and it draws them to the bakery to get some. And that's what it should be with the church. Our unity and our love for one another, when others see it, should be an aroma that draws them to Jesus Christ.

In John 17, with the shadow of the cross hanging over Him, Jesus made it very clear what His desire was for His people. Over and over, He prayed that they may be one, just as He and His Father are one. Jesus then added something very interesting in verse 21, 'That the world may believe that You have sent Me.'

Our unity or disunity will actually affect the world outside. When they see how much we love each other, and our attitude towards one other, they will discover that this thing is for real. They will perhaps want to know more about this Saviour Whom we mention so often. But when we are divided and there is friction among us, then we hear that well-worn phrase, *'Well, there's Christianity for you.'*

Our unity makes us authentic to the world. The world is watching us day by day. When we aren't displaying unity, the world can see right through us. May we never through disunity give the outside world an opportunity to blaspheme God, but rather, may they smell a sweet aroma that leads them to follow the 'scent' and find Jesus.

DAY 48

The Location Of Worship

But the hour comes, and now is, when the true worshippers
shall worship the Father in spirit and in truth:
for the Father seeks such to worship Him.
John 4:23

There is a TV programme in the UK called, *Location, location, location.* When it comes to worship, it is all about location. What do I mean?

In the Old Testament, worship of God centred in a tent, and then a building (a temple). That continued until Jesus came and restored worship back to where it originally was meant to be. *Location: the heart.* You see, in the past, many times God's people had gathered in a location where they worshipped with their mouths and lips, yet their hearts were far from Him. And so, Jesus says that the heart is where worship really takes place, and only when it is done in Spirit and in truth.

So often we think that worship is confined to Sunday mornings and evenings in a church building. Worshipping in Spirit and in truth, with its location in the heart, can happen anywhere: in your home; in work; as you walk along the street; anywhere at all. Hebrews 13:15 tells us that our worship should be continual. So, if it only takes place in church, you would have to be in church all the time to have continual worship! But it's in the heart, and when we get a hold of that, I believe it will transform us.

Worship of course is much more than praise; worship is a lifestyle, and we should offer up worship through our lives. Romans 12:1 tells us to present our bodies as a living sacrifice. Worship comes through consecrating our hands, our feet, our mouths, our bodies, our lives to God, in one continual act of worship. Paul says in 1st Corinthians 10:31 that whatever you do, may you do it to the glory of God. Worship occurs when we seek for God to be glorified through our lives, and it all flows out from the heart.

DAY 49

Give Him The Glory

Give to the LORD the glory due to His name: bring an offering,
and come before Him: worship the LORD in the beauty of holiness.
1st Chronicles 16:29

Sometimes you may hear someone coming out of a church service and saying, 'Huh, I didn't get much out of that!' The question that they should really be asking is, 'What did I *put into* today's service? Did I spectate or participate?'

We don't come to worship God primarily to receive, although it should be added here that we *do* receive. Some people take it to the other extreme, where you would almost think you won't receive anything from God when you worship. God loves to bless His people when they meet together in worship. Having said that, primarily our purpose for worship is to *give* to Him.

Our verse today says to give to the Lord the glory due to His Name. Is the Lord worthy of praise? Is glory and honour due to His holy Name? Then we should give it to Him.

So often as humans, we need to literally bring ourselves kicking and screaming back to the heart of worship (Jesus). It's easy to make it all about *me*. It must be *my* style of music, it must be *my* type of songs, it must revolve around satisfying the way *I* think it should be, or else I cannot participate or enjoy. But if we are letting these things cloud our vision of Jesus, then we've missed out on worshipping Him. We've missed out on giving Him our true worship.

What sort of giving should our worship be? Isaac Watts put it this way: 'Love so amazing, so divine, demands my soul, my life my all.' If our worship feels a bit dry, then we need to get a fresh look at Jesus on the cross. It is here surely that our heartstrings get tuned up and will overflow in a symphony of praise.

Give what is due to His Name, and don't hold back!

DAY 50

What's The Time?

And that, knowing the time, that now it is high time to awake out of sleep: for now is our salvation nearer than when we believed.
Romans 13:11

When I was in primary school, my teacher was perplexed as to why I always got the answers wrong when it came to telling the time. Soon she realised it was because the clocks in our house were deliberately set fifteen minutes fast! Granny McKinley always set them that way so that we wouldn't be late going anywhere. But it didn't work in any case because we always knew subconsciously that we had an extra fifteen minutes to spare. This, then, was the reason why I couldn't tell the time.

Paul declares in Romans 13 that we should know the time. The Greek word here for '*know*' doesn't mean something that you have been taught, but something you know through intuition. In other words, the Holy Spirit bears witness with your spirit as to the serious times in which we live. We read in 1st Chronicles 12:32 that the children of Issachar were men who had an understanding of the times. They read the times just like you would read a book.

In our verse, Paul is basically telling us that it's time to wake up and be alert. We should know the times we are living in and that Jesus' Return is nearer than ever. We are to anticipate and expect Jesus' Return. In the times of the early Christians, when they were persecuted by the Romans, they used the word '*Maranatha*.' It was a common greeting between believers, but also became like a (sort of) password with which to recognise other believers in those dangerous times. It meant, '*Come O Lord.*' They desperately waited and hoped for their Lord to Return.

It wouldn't be out of place if we, as believers, began to stir each other up when we greet or leave each other by saying '*Maranatha*', and meaning it. A church in expectation. A church in readiness. A church that is awake. Can you and I be that church?

DAY 51

Focused Worship

And, behold, a woman in the city, which was a sinner,
when she knew that Jesus sat at meat in the Pharisee's house,
brought an alabaster box of ointment.
Luke 7:37

The simplest definition of the word *'worship'* would be to *'ascribe worth.'* In this fascinating encounter from Luke 7, we have two people who have different estimations as to Jesus' worth. And it isn't what you would expect. This woman in the passage was seen by everyone else as a great sinner, and would have been shunned by many there. Yet she is the one who seems to have the highest estimation of Jesus in the whole room. She pours out her worship to Jesus by washing His feet with her tears, kissing His feet and anointing them with ointment.

Then we come to Simon, who is a highly religious man. He is the one whom you would expect to esteem Jesus with the proper worth He deserves. But Simon doesn't give any water for Jesus' feet; no welcoming kiss; and no oil for His head. These were all basic practices that would have been carried out for any rabbi, let alone for God in the flesh. Simon's worship was non-existent.

This woman's heart was broken and humble. Simon's heart was hard and bitter. She was totally focused on Jesus alone; he was fixated on what he perceived as this woman's sins, while not realising his own sin in not giving Jesus *any* worship. Simon's is a classic example of hypocrisy; a trap into which it is all too easy for anyone to fall. We should always be very wary of criticising anyone else's worship of Jesus. Maybe we think someone is being 'over the top' in their worship. This woman, with her expensive ointment and constant weeping, could have been accused of 'showing off' in her worship; but all Jesus saw was a broken and loving heart. He accepted her worship. When we begin to criticise others' worship, we maybe have lost our focus on Jesus. May God give us a heart of true worship as we pour out our love to Him.

DAY 52

Camel Soup

You blind guides, which strain at a gnat, and swallow a camel.
Matthew 23:24

A man orders some soup and later calls the waiter. The waiter says, 'Yes sir, how can I help?' He replies, 'What is this fly doing in my soup?' The waiter answers, 'It looks like he's doing the breaststroke sir!' (Sorry, that's an old joke!) So, the waiter gets a small sieve and strains at the soup until he removes the offender. With the tiny fly gone, the diner proceeds to eat his soup, but he swallows part of a camel! (Camel soup was on the menu). A big camel hump stuck in his throat and nearly choked him.

The first part I told you about the fly doing the breaststroke was a joke, but the swallowing of the camel hump *wasn't* really a joke. It was based on an illustration similar to what Jesus used in Matthew 23:24, where He said that the Pharisees strained at a fly and swallowed a camel. They made a big fuss over small, insignificant, man-made rules with which they burdened the people, while ignoring the important things that God wanted them to obey.

We saw yesterday that Simon the Pharisee was getting all worked up because this woman, whom he saw as a great sinner, was anointing Jesus' feet with precious ointment and wiping them with her tears. As Simon stood there trying to strain the fly out of her ointment (forgive the double pun), he was swallowing the proverbial camel. Sure, this woman had broken a couple of cultural rules but at least she had got her priorities right in recognising Jesus as God and in worshipping Him. Simon completely failed to give any worship at all to Jesus. He was pointing the finger at this woman, yet there were four others pointing back at Simon. It is so easy for us to see small faults in others while not recognizing big problems in our own hearts. May God give us the grace to see our own blind spots. Let us pray today with the words of Psalm 139:23, 'Search me, O God, and know my heart.'

DAY 53

Worshipping In Difficult Times

And said, Naked came I out of my mother's womb, and naked shall I
return there: the LORD gave, and the LORD has taken away;
blessed be the name of the LORD.
Job 1:21

Sometimes, we think we can only worship God when things are going well; but when things go against us it seems like the wind has been taken from our sails, and we are deflated. Yet, in the Bible time and time again, we discover that some of the greatest worship comes from the greatest pain. Look at Job: in the space of one day, he loses his servants, possessions, animals, sons, and daughters. He gets up, shaves his head, falls to the ground, and worships. *Wow!* He says, 'The Lord gave, and the Lord has taken away; blessed be the Name of the Lord.' That was his reaction as the last piece of bad news came to him about his sons and daughters. In all honesty, could we have done it so readily? But Job falls on the ground and worships God.

In Genesis 22, Abraham is on his way to sacrifice his son Isaac. You know the one who had been promised to him as the beginning of a great multitude of nations? Yes, that one. Abraham tells the other men to stay there while he goes with Isaac to worship. *Wow,* again! The man is no doubt going through inner turmoil, yet he says he is going to *worship*. The woman from Luke 7, whom we have been looking at, had a life that was broken and bruised. Yet in her sadness, as she comes and worships Jesus, something beautiful breaks out from inside her heart. It is an overflowing of worship and, in the midst of it all, she finds peace.

How many times have you walked into church and felt that you couldn't really worship because of some difficult things that have happened during the week? But you pushed through the pain barrier, and gave Jesus your sacrifice of praise. What happened? You went out a different person than when you first came in. When we engage in worship, something wonderful takes place.

DAY 54

The Fridge Is Always Full

Pray without ceasing.
1st Thessalonians 5:17

Have you ever been hungry, raided the fridge, and the particular food you were looking for isn't there? Or even worse, there is nothing there at all? Recently, I bought my favourite honey-roasted ham chunks. I went later to eat them, my taste buds being all set for a tasty treat, only to discover my eldest girl had eaten them! All she could offer was a feeble *'sorry'*!

What happens when you start to think this way about prayer? That every time I open the 'fridge door', there's going to be nothing there? Prayer doesn't seem to be working? I would guess that at some stage of our lives, we have all had that thought or been tempted to think it.

If, when coming down to the fridge and finding no ham, I said, *'There's never anything here when I want it,'* that statement would not be true. Maybe, once or twice at most, the thing isn't there that I'm looking for, but most of the time the fridge is well stocked up.

Sometimes, when one or two prayers don't seem to be answered (the way we want them to), we make a blanket statement that prayer doesn't work. *'I never seem to get any answers.'* But that's also not true. God answers our prayers every day. He has given us family and friends, food on our tables, and clothes on our backs. He has protected, guided, and blessed us more than we will ever know. Our 'spiritual fridge' is always full!

Now and again, when the fridge doesn't have what *we want*, we don't throw the fridge out. Now and again, when prayers don't seem to be answered the way we think they should, don't throw prayer out. Prayer works. But not always the way we want it, or when we want it. Keep praying.

DAY 55

Traffic Lights

*Wait on the LORD: be of good courage, and He shall
strengthen your heart: wait, I say, on the LORD.*
Psalm 27:14

Prayer can be like traffic lights. Sometimes, it's a *'go';*
sometimes it's a *'wait,'* and other times it's a big red *'stop.'*
Sometimes, we think that all of God's answers to our best
prayers have to be *'go,'* and we find it hard to take a *'wait'* or a
'stop.' I like what somebody said about prayer, and while it's
perhaps not a perfect statement, I think it is generally a good gauge
to go by. When the prayer is wrong, or not His will, God says *'no.'*
When the prayer is right, but the timing is wrong, God says *'slow'*
(or wait). When the prayer is right, and the timing is right, God
says *'go.'*

Israel longed for the Messiah, which was a good desire, but the
wrong timing. They waited centuries for their Messiah. Did God
not love them because He didn't answer their cry immediately?
Oh, He loved them. But the Bible says in Galatians 4:4, that at the
appointed time (God's time), God sent forth His Son.

And then one day, for people like Anna and Simeon at the temple,
who were praying for their Messiah to come; that particular day,
they not only prayed the right prayer, but it was also the appointed
time.

God's delays are not always denials. Sometimes, they can be.
Sometimes, He does say *'no,'* and we don't understand, but He
knows best. He is the perfect One Who knows every circumstance,
every heart, and every future. He knows things that we do not even
begin to understand. However, Psalm 27:14 encourages us to wait
on the Lord. When we pray, we are waiting upon the Lord. The
verse says that when we wait upon the Lord, He will strengthen
our hearts. Whether the answer is, *'yes,'* *'wait,'* or *'no,'* you can be
assured that if you wait on Him, He will give you the strength to
accept whatever His answer is.

DAY 56

Remember His Words

Remember the word that I said to you, The servant is not greater than his lord. If they have persecuted Me, they will also persecute you; if they have kept My saying, they will keep yours also.
John 15:20

I was preparing a sermon on a beautiful morning. The window was open and I could smell a lovely barbeque. Every now and again, I wondered who would be having a barbeque so early in the morning. This went on for a while. Then, I suddenly panicked. I had just remembered Di's words as she was walking out the door. Yes, she distinctly said, *'Will you turn off the mince after ten minutes?'* In my defence, once you get lost in a sermon, you don't notice time passing! I ran downstairs and tried to salvage it, but the meat was completely burned. It was beyond even the redemption of a rich tomato bolognaise sauce to disguise the taste! All because I didn't remember Di's words as she went out the door.

In John 15, Jesus was soon to make an exit, not through an earthly door, but was soon to ascend through a Heavenly door. Jesus gave instructions to His disciples before leaving and asked them to remember His Word that He had spoken to them. Since He was persecuted, so they would be also. The reason for this would be *because of His Name.* (v 20-21) Often when going through life, we forget Jesus' Words. When we feel alone, we can forget that He said He will never leave us. We can forget that He said worrying cannot change one thing in our lives. We can forget that He has told us not to be troubled, for He is coming again for us.

Did the disciples remember what Jesus said? It seems they did. When persecution came in the book of Acts, they fearlessly preached in the Name of Jesus. The icing on the cake, though, came in Acts 5 when, after being brought before the Sanhedrin, they left that place rejoicing that they had been counted worthy to suffer disgrace *for Jesus' Name!* They remembered His Words. Which of the Lord's Words does He want us to remember today?

DAY 57

The Missionary God

And he called his ten servants, and delivered them ten pounds,
and said to them, Occupy till I come.
Luke 19:13

A friend phoned me one day to inform me that he was at a train station which was a bit of a distance from his intended destination. I asked him what had happened. He said that he had fallen asleep and missed the train stop! We had a laugh about it.

However, sometimes we can treat mission a bit like a train ticket. We have our 'ticket to Heaven' and are just sitting back and enjoying the ride. In some cases, we are even falling asleep on the train, while oblivious to everything going on around us. It seems we are happy with that until we reach our destination, which is Heaven. We go to church and worship the Lord, but we don't really have a burden for the lost souls of men and women.

We wrongly interpret Jesus' Words to 'Occupy till I come,' as meaning to fill up the space and don't budge! But the word 'occupy' here means to 'be busy' until He comes.

God is a missionary God, and someone has said that the first mission headquarters were in Heaven. The first missionary that was ever sent was Jesus. He was officially commissioned long before the foundation of the world. The church has been commissioned to be a missionary church right from its inception. You have maybe heard it said before, that mission is the lifeblood of the church, and it is so true. Without mission, the church and the individual Christian have lost their vision and focus.

We are here for mission: to win the lost, to go out into the highways and byways, and to bring them in. We are to be proactive and not reactive. We are to be intentional rather than accidental in our mission. Go into all the world and preach the gospel.

DAY 58

A Missionary Mindset

And Moses said to God, Who am I, that I should go to Pharaoh,
and that I should bring forth the children of Israel out of Egypt?
Exodus 3:11

I once heard the late Derek Bingham suggest that when Moses was called to deliver Israel, in effect his reply to God was, 'Here I am, send *Aaron*.' That statement always stayed with me. Sometimes we think that everybody else is called, except us. However, if you are saved, then you are a missionary. It's not just that person who is serving God in Africa, India or China, but it is also you and me. Maybe you have seen missionary reports and you have thought that you would have loved to have been a missionary, but you never felt the call. However, you can be a missionary exactly where you are right now.

Paul spoke about the love of Christ which *constrained* him to do certain things for the Lord. (2nd Corinthians 5:14) The love of Christ should also constrain and grip us because we have been recipients of this love. You have probably heard the saying (usually attributed to D.T. Niles) that evangelism is just one beggar telling another beggar where to find bread. And that is simply what mission also is.

Think about this. A doctor works with patients; that is their focus. A mechanic works with people whose cars need to be fixed; that is their focus. A dentist works with people who have problems with their teeth. Again, that is their focus. If we are missionaries (and each one of us is), then our focus should be on *lost people*, while thinking and praying about how we are going to reach them for Jesus Christ.

We need to get into this missionary mindset. I am a missionary. '*Who me?*' '*Yes, you!*' '*Here I am then. Don't send Aaron! I'll gladly go!*'

DAY 59

Playing By Ear

Now when they had gone throughout Phrygia and the region of Galatia,
and were forbidden of the Holy Ghost to preach the word in Asia,
Acts 16:6

When I was at Primary School, I (briefly) took up playing the violin. After a while, the music teacher told my mum that I was playing 'by ear' and not by the music. I would have to stop my lessons unless I would play by the music. In front of my mum, she got me to play a new piece. I couldn't really play it properly as I hadn't heard that piece before. I was relying on playing 'by ear'. That was the end of my violin music lessons.

However, with mission, we don't play it 'by ear'. There is a clear and distinct director of missions, and He is the Holy Spirit. It has been said that the Acts of the Apostles should really be called the *Book of the Acts of the Holy Spirit through the Apostles*. The apostles completely relied on the Holy Spirit.

When we 'do mission', whether it be at home, or abroad, it's vital that we go in the direction and the power of the Holy Spirit. To leave the Holy Spirit out of it is to invite disaster. It is like trying to chop down an oak tree with a penknife. You have no power with a pen knife but, when you take a chain-saw, then you have power. We must invite the Holy Spirit to direct us.

Paul had his plans to go into Asia with the gospel but at that particular time, the Holy Spirit forbade it. Paul had good intentions, but it was the wrong time. Then, he came to Mysia, intending to go to Bithynia, but again, the Holy Spirit said *no*. There was a reason for this. When he came to Troas, Paul had a vision of a man in Macedonia from whom he received a call. We know of the great things that happened subsequently in Philippi. Two doors closed, but *the door* opened that God wanted Paul to walk through. Are we sensitive to the guidance of the Holy Spirit?

DAY 60

Opening Prison Doors

And a certain woman named Lydia, a seller of purple, of the city of Thyatira, which worshipped God, heard us: whose heart the Lord opened, that she attended to the things which were spoken of Paul.
Acts 16:14

We saw yesterday how Paul's journey to Macedonia, and particularly Philippi, was a result of the Holy Spirit closing one door and opening up a different one. The crowning glory of this chapter, Acts 16, is of course, when prison doors swing wide open due to an earthquake. In a way, it can be seen as representative of what happens spiritually in this chapter, when the prison doors for three human hearts are opened, bringing liberty and salvation through Jesus.

The first prison door was the prison of *religion*. Lydia originally came from Thyatira in Asia, 240 miles away from Philippi. Yet she has a divine appointment with Paul, who has just been told not to go to Asia, but to Philippi! God's sovereignty brings these two together. This is no chance meeting. Thank God for divine appointments in our lives. It seems Lydia had been a convert to Judaism, but we read that she was a woman 'Whose heart the Lord opened.' Thank God, He can break through the traditions and deadness of religion, opening prison doors and setting people free.

The second prison door was the prison of *control*. A demon-possessed girl was being controlled and manipulated by her 'owners', a picture of each life without Jesus, which is controlled by the god of this world. We read that Paul was grieved by this (as we should be also when we see lost souls) and that she was set free in the Name of Jesus. God still opens the prison doors of captivity in people's lives today. The final prison was the prison of *hopelessness*. Here was a big, tough jailer who is about to kill himself, until he hears the beautiful Words of the gospel, 'Believe on the Lord Jesus Christ, and you shall be saved' (Acts 16:31). Whatever the bondage, Jesus still opens prison doors today!

DAY 61

Blessing Blockers

*And Terah took Abram his son, and Lot the son of Haran his son's son,
and Sarai his daughter in law, his son Abram's wife; and they went forth
with them from Ur of the Chaldees, to go into the land of Canaan;
and they came to Haran, and dwelt there.*
Genesis 11:31

Abraham seemed to have unwittingly removed himself temporarily from the authority of God, and had placed himself under the authority of his father. He had placed a yoke upon himself.

Notice the wording: 'Terah *took* Abram his son,' etc., from Ur of the Chaldees.' Terah *took* his son. That wasn't the way it was supposed to happen. God told Abraham to leave his country, his kindred, and his father's house. Abraham was to be the one who was meant to be leading himself and Sarah out of Ur, but here it is Terah doing the leading.

Due to Terah's leading, they end up settling in Haran. God had never called Abraham to Haran. Abraham had placed himself under the yoke of his idol-worshipping father, whom God had told him to leave.

Actually, Abraham had a two-fold yoke: not only Terah, his father, but Lot also was weighing Abraham down. They were keeping him back from the full blessing. Terah and Lot were *blessing blockers.*
I wonder, are there any blessing blockers in our lives? I wonder, are we sleepwalking into situations that are making us captive to someone or something else? Are we taking counsel from other people who are leading us away from getting closer to God? Let us be careful not to put a yoke upon ourselves.

Break that yoke off, put things right with the Lord, and watch the blessing being released over your life in God's timing.

DAY 62

Breakthrough!

And the LORD said to Abram, after that Lot was separated from him,
Lift up now your eyes, and look from the place where you are
northward, and southward, and eastward, and westward.
Genesis 13:14

In Abraham's and Lot's lives, there comes a point when the herdsmen on each side can't get along together; and Genesis 13 tells us that the two groups deliberately separate from each other. Once they separate, Abraham's blessing explodes like fireworks. It's taken a long time. Having been told to separate from his country and his people, Abraham has been delayed in Haran with his father. Lot was also tagging along, but now Abraham has put things right.

What do we read next? Abraham settled in the land of Canaan. He was now where God wanted him to be. You too can also get back to where God wants you to be in your relationship with Him if you surrender whatever it is that is holding you back.

We then read that the Lord told Abram (and we are reminded that it is 'after Lot had *separated* from him,') to lift up his eyes towards all the land that he could see and He would give it to his offspring forever, making them as innumerable as the dust on the earth. But this reconfirmation of God's promise didn't come until the last tie was broken; when Terah and Lot were out of the picture. Abraham's blessing had finally broken through.

While everything which we receive from God comes by grace and not through our 'performance', yet we can sometimes hold back blessings due to our disobedience, or by detouring from God's direction for our lives. Someone reading these words, I pray, is going to step out in obedience to what the Lord has instructed them to do. They are going to give themselves wholly to God and, in His time, should expect a spiritual breakthrough.

DAY 63

Bursting With Blessings

*Blessed be the God and Father of our Lord Jesus Christ, who has
blessed us with all spiritual blessings in heavenly places in Christ.*
Ephesians 1:3

Ephesians Chapter 1 is absolutely bursting with blessings. The truth expressed there is something that we have to live, breathe and understand. It is vital for the spiritual life. If you have to read this chapter every morning just to get its truths into your soul, then do it. I believe it is *that* important as we are reminded of just who we are in Christ and the blessings that He has brought to our lives.

To go out in the morning knowing that you are blessed, chosen, adopted, accepted, redeemed, forgiven, a grace receiver, an inheritor, and sealed with the Spirit, will give you confidence and peace of mind as you start your day. It will give you a sure foundation for whatever comes your way. Satan doesn't want you to read Ephesians 1 and to live in the certainty of it. He wants you to go into this week thinking that God has forgotten about you and that the future for you is dark.

Do you know where the book of Ephesians was written? It was most likely written when Paul was under house arrest in Rome. Now, if we were in that situation and writing a letter to the Ephesians, what would we write about? Maybe complain about the food and living conditions? Ask when was anyone going to get around to bailing us out of this place?

But Paul's letter is bursting with praise for his God. And this teaches us that praise doesn't just come from places of beauty, but that it can overflow even inside a place of confinement.

I want to encourage you today that from behind the 'prison cell' of the circumstances of life in which you find yourself, praise can rise as you remember the blessings that you have been brought into through Jesus Christ.

DAY 64

The End Of An Era

The grass withers, the flower fades:
but the word of our God shall stand for ever.
Isaiah 40:8

In May 2021, the last lilac tree from mum's house blew down in a storm. It had been there since before mum had moved into the house in 1954, blossoming, and full of lilac. Passers-by used to ask if they could take some lilac home. The tree had endured storms for over 70 years, through our childhood and growing up, still standing strong. I remember one particular time when Granda Seifert went to cut some lilac. He got up a ladder, lifted his arms, and had forgotten that he had loosened his braces after dinner. You can guess what happened next, as Granny Seifert let out a yelp of laughter! Those were the days. But last year, a strong wind finally brought the tree down. I felt sad when it was gone. It was like the end of an era.

Just short of a year later, on 11th April 2022, mum went to be with the Lord. Just like the old faithful lilac tree, mum had withstood life's storms (through her trust in Jesus), for 82 years of her life. Although we know that Mum and Dad are now both together in Heaven, for my sister, Lynne, and myself, it is the end of an era. We can, however, hold on to happy memories, and look forward to being reunited with them both one day.

Perhaps you have come to places in your life where a chapter has closed. Maybe it's a loved one who has passed on, or a job which you had for years has ended. Life is an ever-changing cycle. They say that time waits for no-one. As chapters close in our lives, we are reminded by today's verse that the grass withers and the flower fades, but the Word of our God stands forever. Throughout the changing scenes of your life, the promises of God never change. The best way to deal with these changing seasons is to obtain strength and comfort from the changeless Word of God. Why not pick it up right now, and receive some changeless promises?

DAY 65

Hear And Grow

And He said to them, Take heed what you hear:
with what measure you mete, it shall be measured to you:
and to you that hear shall more be given.
Mark 4:24

Take heed of what you hear. '*Take heed*' is strong wording. It means that we need to pay careful attention to something and get a grasp of what it means. Don't be a casual listener to the Word of God; every Word of God is precious. It is like gold and we are responsible for how we treat His Word.

Jesus says that in regard to hearing; depending on how well we hear, then it shall be measured back to us. Biblical hearing does not solely involve what enters through the ear, but includes seeking to understand and discern through the guidance of the Holy Spirit what is being said. When we seek to do this, then we can expect to benefit spiritually. Subsequently, if we don't study the Word much, we should not expect to get much benefit from it.

We thank the Lord for His Grace, which pours blessings upon us even when we have been slack in our attention to His Word; but Jesus is definitely teaching here that we can't arrogantly *expect* to be blessed if we are not paying close attention to God's Word. Martha, one particular day, didn't put much stock in hearing from Jesus and understanding what He was saying, so she couldn't really have expected to receive many benefits. But Mary sat at His feet and listened to every Word. She wanted to learn more from the Master.

Finally, it says that to those who hear, *more* shall be given. Sounds to me like there's some sort of blessing promised here! The more you listen to the Lord and hear from Him, the more you can expect Him to open up your understanding, and for you to increase in spiritual wisdom. What an incentive.

Do you desire more of God? Pay special attention to His Words and in understanding them. You will never regret it.

DAY 66

Follow Me

And He says to them, Follow Me, and I will make you fishers of men.
Matthew 4:19

What is discipleship about? It's about two words: *'Follow Me.'* Forgetting this truth is where we lose our focus sometimes. Being a disciple is simply following Christ. 'Follow Me.'

Don't follow a system; follow Him. Don't follow a religion; follow Him. Don't follow a set of traditions set down by man; follow Him. Don't follow your own opinions; follow Him.

Christ is our goal, our prize, our example, our leader, and our all in all. Focus on Jesus. Paul said, 'That I may *know* Him' (Philippians 3:10). Our whole Christian life is taken up with knowing Jesus better, and being more like Him. Satan will do anything and everything to get your focus off Jesus and to divert you from following Him. Satan can be so subtle and he can get you in a place where it seems you are doing religious things, where it seems you are doing activities for Jesus, and even working for Him. However, your focus may not be on Jesus. It may be that you aren't really, as such, following Him or depending totally upon Him. Sometimes, it is a good thing to just take a step back and look at our lives, and ask this simple question: *am I following Him*? Have I got distracted along the way from the simplicity, reality, and passion of following Jesus?

He leads and we follow. When we are following Jesus, we are no longer following our own desires. When you follow someone there is movement. We should never be stuck in the same place. In what direction is Jesus moving us? He is always moving us onwards, and closer to Himself. Are we allowing Him to draw us deeper, and guide us to the places He wants us to be in our lives?

Let's just get rid of all the complications, and our own ideas, and our own will, and let's get back to the basics. *'Follow Me.'*

DAY 67

Two Deaths

And He said to them all, If any man will come after Me,
let him deny himself, and take up his cross daily, and follow Me.
Luke 9:23

We tend to change the meaning of this verse. Maybe we have been feeling a bit under the weather, and we say, 'Well, we all have our cross to bear.' Or maybe we are put on a shift at work with someone whom we don't really get along with, and we sarcastically say, 'We all have our cross to bear!' That's not what this verse means. What does it mean then? In Jesus' time, to carry your cross was never seen as being symbolic of the burdens that we bear, or the difficult situations we go through. There was only one meaning to this. To carry your cross meant you were going to your death, and one of the most cruel deaths at that.

Jesus is telling us that if we want to be His disciples, we have to deny ourselves, and take up our cross. Deitrich Bonhoeffer, the German pastor and theologian who was put to death by the Nazis, said this: 'When Christ calls a man, he bids him come and die.' We shouldn't see this as something to dread, but rather as something that brings us into a place of victory. We are simply crowning Jesus as Lord of our lives, of our finances, plans, future, and our thoughts. Essentially, I have died and Jesus lives in me.

There are Christians that you have come across in life and there's something really different about them: the way they react to things, the way they talk; the way they are so selfless; the way they 'carry themselves' and the way they are so Christ-like. They, of course, are not perfect, but there's just generally something different about them that stands out. How did they come to that place? Did it just suddenly happen? No, they have gone through a process of dying to self and allowing Jesus to live through them. Salvation requires one death (Jesus' death on the cross). But true discipleship requires two deaths. Having been saved already through *His death*, true discipleship requires *death to self*. He bids us to come and die.

DAY 68

Disciples Make Disciples

Go you therefore, and teach all nations, baptizing them
in the name of the Father, and of the Son, and of the Holy Ghost:
Matthew 28:19

You may have heard the saying that 'disciples make disciples, who make disciples,' and so on. The problem is that so often, when people are converted, we (the church) encourage them to stay inside the four walls, while listening comfortably to the Word preached and taught. It is necessary, of course, for them to hear and learn. However, we should encourage disciples to go outside the four walls and make other disciples, in whatever sphere of influence they find themselves. I wonder how many Christians have become spectators, who just watch what goes on in church, and they feel a little frustrated. You see, we can become frustrated when we restrict ourselves to being solely inside the four walls of a church because we weren't made for that!

We recently bought some pet fish for the kids: three guppies, and four neon tetras. Sometimes, I feel sorry for them when I see them swimming around the four sides of the small fish tank. They weren't really made for that. They were made to be free. Similarly, we who have been made disciples by Jesus have this desire within us to make other disciples because we are so grateful for what He has done in our lives. Yet we will feel frustrated when we restrict ourselves to the four walls of the church. Just like the fish in the tank, we get used to it. One of the first things that the woman of Samaria did was to run back to her town, bursting to tell others, so they could be disciples, too. When you have been set free, you can't wait to tell others how *they* can be set free; it's just natural.

It's time to break free and break out for Jesus. It's wonderful to be part of His great commission. Your gifting, personality, and talents are unique to you. Only you can do what God has created you to do. Be the person whom He has called you to be, and go make disciples, who make disciples, who make disciples.

DAY 69

The Real Thing

Then said Jesus to those Jews which believed on Him,
If you continue in My word, then are you My disciples indeed.
John 8:31

We have all heard of the slogan, '*It's the real thing*', which belongs to *Coca-Cola*. Some have tried to copy their drink. You could set three or four similar brands in unmarked glasses and, if you were to taste each one, you would most likely know straight away which was the one that is associated with being *the real thing,* due to its distinct taste.

But how do you know if someone is a true disciple, or *the real thing*? In John 6, we read about those who seemed to be disciples, yet they had now turned their backs on Jesus. How do you tell the difference between the real and the false? Jesus answers the question for us in our verse. Those who are His disciples continue in His Word. That is the true test. The Bible never encourages us to rely solely on past experiences. Yes, it is necessary to be able to look back at that moment when you started the journey with Jesus; but the test of the genuineness of that experience is your continuation in His Word *today.* Disciples are those who trust and obey and continue. Even when the going gets tough.

Maybe today, you feel as if you have drifted away slightly. Or maybe you have been away from God for a longer period. One single moment can change all that forever. Just come back to Him today, ask forgiveness for the past, and from this moment onwards you can continue in His Word.

Maybe you have been having it tough recently and have been thinking of giving up. Hebrews 12:1 mentions a cloud of witnesses around us. It seems they are the great characters from the '*Hall of Faith*' in Chapter 11. Noah, Abraham, Moses, Gideon, and David would all witness to you today. They had it tough. At times, they seemed broken. But they continued in His Word. And they would call you today to keep on going. It will be worth it all.

DAY 70

The Weapon Of Praise

And the children of Israel arose, and went up to the house of God,
and asked counsel of God, and said, Which of us shall go up first
to the battle against the children of Benjamin?
And the LORD said, Judah shall go up first.
Judges 20:18

Judah means *'praise'*. His name came about in the middle of heartbreak and sorrow. Leah was one of Jacob's two wives and took second place to Rachel. In Genesis 29 we read three times that she gave birth, and each time she gave her sons names that expressed her sorrow that Jacob didn't seem to love her the way he loved Rachel. But then she gives birth to another son; and this time, as she names him, there is no mention of her sorrow. She called him Judah, and she says, 'Now will I praise the Lord.' Leah found out that, even when life squeezed her to the max, ultimately it squeezed praise out of her lips. It may not have come immediately (she had to wait until her fourth son), but it did come. Many times, when heartache comes our way, we find it hard to praise. But if you keep holding the hand of God, you will find that one day, you will praise once again like Leah, even in the midst of your heartache.

The children of Israel in Judges 20 had to face a battle and they asked the Lord which tribe should lead them. The Lord said that Judah would go up first. Remember what Judah means? *Praise!* Now I'm not suggesting that, if you just simply sing, then all of your troubles will disappear. No. What I am suggesting is that, when we praise the Lord, we are taking Biblical truths upon our lips and hearts and the Holy Spirit can use them to bring us strength and hope as we face the battles of life. Praise also takes the focus off ourselves and puts it onto the Lord.

When we think about the battles we are facing, it can so easily fill us with fear. How will you face your battles today? Put *'Praise the Lord'* at the front of the battle and go in His strength today.

DAY 71

What A Friend

Hereafter I call you not servants; for the servant knows not what his lord does: but I have called you friends; for all things that I have heard of My Father I have made known to you.
John 15:15

There have been many titles given to Jesus in the Scriptures; but there is one title that is given to Him by men which is meant to be an insult, yet to the soul that longs to be free, this is one of the most encouraging titles that a sinner could hear. Jesus was called, a *'Friend of sinners.'* How amazing it is, that we, who were once the enemies of God, can be the friends of God. We read in James 2:23 that Abraham was called the friend of God. I wonder what they talked about? Proverbs 18:24 speaks of a friend that sticks closer than a brother. Surely there can never be a friend like Jesus; a friend Who can never let us down, and always has our best interests at heart.

Jesus' friendship, of course, is different from all other friendships. Most friendships don't really cost us anything, except when a buddy says, 'I forgot my wallet again, can you get the coffee this time round?' However, the cost of this friendship with Jesus Christ is beyond calculation. Many times, we unthinkingly sing Joseph Scriven's hymn, 'What a Friend we have in Jesus,' and forget the price that was paid for that friendship. It cost the precious Blood of Jesus Christ. 'Greater love has no man than this, that a man lay down his life for his friends' (John 15:13). Yet we were the enemies of God. What a love, and at such a cost.

In John 15:15, Jesus says, 'I have called you friends.' I am a friend of God. I don't rub shoulders with the presidents of this world. The closest I have got to anyone famous was to shake a well-known politician's hand; I attended church with a converted pop-star, and I have worked alongside two Irish league footballers! I don't really know anyone famous, influential or powerful in this world, but Jesus Christ says of me (and of you), 'I have called you friends.'

DAY 72

A New Dimension Of Faith

The impotent man answered Him, Sir, I have no man, when the water is
troubled, to put me into the pool: but while I am coming,
another steps down before me.
John 5:7

In John 5:6 we read that Jesus saw this disabled man sitting by the pool of Bethesda. He caught Jesus' attention. And the Lord also sees you, His child, today. You are not anonymous to Him. He sees you in your pain and knows what you are going through. Jesus asks the man if he wants to be healed. It may seem like a strange question, but here was a man who had been like this for thirty-eight years and his hopes had been buried a long time ago. What Jesus did was to awaken hope in his heart again.

What Jesus does next is to take this man into a new dimension of faith. Up until now, in this man's mind, the only way he could be healed would be for someone to bring him to the pool when the waters were moved by an angel. In addition to that, he had to be the first one in, or else he couldn't be healed, and he points this out to Jesus. But Jesus was now opening his heart to something that he had never even considered before. There are no waters involved, no angel, no help needed from others; just faith in whatever Jesus tells him to do, and he will be healed.

Sometimes, God has to move us into another dimension of faith. *'The only way my son or daughter will ever get their life sorted out is x, y, and z.' 'The only way I can overcome this problem is x, y, and z.'* We have it all worked out in our minds. But today, give that problem over to Jesus and let Him deal with it His way. Naaman thought the only way he could be healed was for the prophet Elisha to come in person and to do some spectacular miracle. Elisha didn't even come personally to greet him, but sent his servant, who told him to dip in the dirty Jordan seven times. God's ways are not always our ways. When we stop putting God 'in a box', then He can draw us into a new dimension of faith.

DAY 73

Filled To The Brim

And to know the love of Christ, which passes knowledge,
that you might be filled with all the fullness of God.
Ephesians 3:19

Have you ever run the car on empty? So often we do it, even though we know that one day we may be caught out. Someday we will get up late and, being in a rush, will start up the car and realise it's empty. As humans, there is something within us that causes us to wait until the last minute to do things. Even now, as I am writing this, our electric meter has sounded the alarm twice, indicating that I have to top up! When the car starts to run low on petrol, a light shows up on the dashboard and, similarly, there are warning signs and sounds which let us know when we are dangerously near to empty in our spiritual lives.

I wonder, are you running on empty, in a spiritual sense? Maybe you have been discouraged, or doubts have entered your mind. Maybe you are being attacked by the forces of darkness; or perhaps you have been working so hard for the Lord that you are burned out. Maybe you have recently been facing a myriad of emotional, physical, and spiritual difficulties. Have the alarm bells been sounding in your life and you know you are at *empty*?

Our verse is about being filled with the fullness of God. *'Filled'*, from the Greek, is to be *'filled to the brim.'* The *'fullness of God'* includes all we need for our spiritual lives. How do we get this? Paul says it is by knowing the love of Christ. The word *'know'* indicates experiential knowledge. While it is vital to read the Bible, we need much more than head knowledge; we need a relational knowledge of Jesus on a daily basis, through His love (Paul is speaking here of *'agape'* love: Jesus' sacrificial love). Are you feeling spiritually empty? Focus on the sacrificial love of Jesus displayed on the cross and let it fill your heart. Walk and talk with Him; rest in Him. As this relationship grows, you will discover that you are being renewed and refilled, yes, even up to the brim!

DAY 74

The Highest Court In The Land

And I saw a great white throne, and Him that sat on it,
from whose face the earth and the heaven fled away;
and there was found no place for them.
Revelation 20:11

On 24th September 2019, all eyes were on the Supreme Court in the UK as a decision was being made regarding the legality of the then Prime Minister, Boris Johnson's prorogation of Parliament. The case had been taken to the high courts in England, Scotland, and Northern Ireland, and now an appeal was being made to the highest court in the land. In the end, they ruled that the prorogation was unlawful.

When we come to Revelation 20, we are reminded that in reality, the Supreme Court is *not* the highest court in the land. The highest court in the land is actually out of this world and in another realm. One day soon that great Court will sit and provide all the evidence of every single thought, motive, word, and deed. There will be no court of appeal, as all those present have already rejected Jesus Christ. It is known as the Great White Throne Judgment and there has never been, nor will there ever be after it, anything like this Court. Every unbeliever since the dawn of time will be there: kings, presidents, celebrities, the rich, and the poor, from all walks of life. A vast array of humanity will be awaiting the final sentence from the Judge that will send them to their final doom. When I think of the horror of that moment, I am reminded of the reported words of an atheist to a Christian. He said something like this: 'If you Christians really believed what you preach, then you would literally crawl over broken glass to even reach one soul and save them from the awfulness of what you are telling us.'

God is not willing that any should perish. Jesus has paid the price to set people free. As we think of those who will stand at that Throne without Jesus, let's determine to seek God's help to win the lost with the great news of the gospel.

DAY 75

Bring It To Jesus

When Jesus then lifted up His eyes, and saw a great company come to Him, He says to Philip, Where shall we buy bread, that these may eat?
John 6:5

Here is an everyday life problem. A lot of people are without any food. Jesus uses this opportunity to test His disciples and to see what they would do. It's a bit like when someone is training for a job, and the person who is training might see a situation, and ask the trainee what they would do in that situation. You see, the disciples still have their '*L*' plates on; they are still learning (and so are we). So, what answers will they come up with?

Peter just sees the financial problem. He's got the 'calculator' out, is adding up the figures, and two plus two definitely isn't adding up to four. Peter is still working in the realm of an earthly solution, rather than a heavenly one. Before we judge Peter, though, we most likely would have done the same!

'But Peter....erm...the answer is standing right beside you!'

Andrew does a little bit better. He has a look to see what exactly they *have* got; he takes inventory and finds a young lad with five barley loaves and two fish. But then he asks, 'What are they among so many?' (verse 8). Well, at least we can commend Andrew for bringing the lad to Jesus.

'Erm.... Andrew.....the answer is standing right beside you!'

If you are taking stock of things in your life, and they *don't* add up (like Peter); or when you go to see what you *have* got, and it's not enough (like Andrew); then bring it to Jesus. That physical, emotional, financial, or spiritual problem: present it to Jesus and say, 'Lord, I'm giving it to You.' And, just like the disciples, although you don't see an earthly answer yet, the answer is not only standing beside you; He is within you, around you, and above you. Bring it to Jesus. He *has* the answer, and He *is* the answer.

DAY 76

Saving Us From Ourselves

And immediately Jesus constrained His disciples to get into a ship,
and to go before Him to the other side,
while He sent the multitudes away.
Matthew 14:22

When Jesus fed the 5,000, the crowd 'sniffed' something out for themselves. If Jesus could feed this crowd using five loaves and two fish, surely then He could defeat their enemies, the Romans? They wanted to make Him king. Matthew and Mark say that Jesus constrained His disciples to go ahead into the ship and sail to the other side while He would disperse the crowd. The word *'constrain'* is a strong word denoting compulsion. I have to constrain my girls to eat their dinner without being distracted, yet I never have to constrain them to eat sweets! Constrain has the thought of trying to get someone to do something they don't really want to do. When Jesus constrained the disciples to leave, the indication was that they didn't really want to go. Some think Jesus was protecting them from being influenced by a crowd that was getting 'whipped up' to proclaim Him as king.

Was Jesus protecting the disciples? Peter was a man of impulse. Would he have been 'whipped up' by the crowd? James and John were called *'sons of thunder.'* You didn't want to mess with them! Among them was Simon *'the Zealot.'* The Zealots were a Jewish group who wanted independence from the Romans. What might these guys have done if they had been caught up in the emotion of it all? They still didn't understand Jesus' real mission. They saw Him as the Messiah Who would deliver them from their enemies, not die on a cross. Was Jesus saving them from themselves? Sometimes, we are determined to go down a particular route and it is our 'flesh' that is guiding us. It seems that God puts obstacle after obstacle in our way to try to save us from ourselves. Is God doing something like that in our lives at the moment? Don't kick against it. Listen to His voice as He constrains us to walk away from it. God's way is the best way.

DAY 77

Jesus Is With You In The Darkness

And entered into a ship, and went over the sea toward Capernaum.
And it was now dark, and Jesus was not come to them.
John 6:17

We saw yesterday that Jesus constrained his disciples to get on a ship. What happens next is that Jesus goes up a mountain alone to pray, while the disciples go by boat towards Capernaum. John tells us that it was now dark and Jesus was not coming to them. I wonder, does that describe your situation today? You are a believer, but the darkness seems to have descended upon your life in whatever shape or form that may be. Then, just as in this verse, not only are things dark, but it seems to you that Jesus has not come to help you. You can't seem to hear Him or feel His Presence in the middle of your darkness.

However, we know that Jesus was up the mountain praying, and no doubt praying for His disciples. Later in Mark, we read that He saw them and the difficulties they were having in rowing their boat on a stormy sea. And so, while they cannot see Jesus, He can see them. He is watching over them and, at the appropriate time, He would make Himself known.

As we face life's storms, we may not always feel His Presence, but He is still there. He is watching over you, His child. Many times, we cannot see or feel the sun on a cloudy day, but it is still there behind the dark clouds. It is said that some writing was found on the wall of a cellar in a World War 2 concentration camp. The unknown writer expressed that they believed in the sun even when it wasn't shining. They believed in love even when no one was there. And they believed in God, even when He seemed silent.

Although it's difficult for us to understand (as humans who rely on the senses of feel and touch), yet we are assured that Jesus is with us *24/7*, not because we 'feel' it, but because His Word declares that He will never leave us nor forsake us. Stand upon His Word even when you don't feel anything. His Word is truth.

DAY 78

It Is I

But He says to them, It is I; be not afraid.
John 6:20

The disciples had rowed between three and four miles and were now roughly in the middle of the lake. They see the figure of someone walking on the water. These seasoned sailors are scared to death. Matthew tells us that the disciples thought it was a spirit. They thought they were seeing something that was going to harm them. The mind can play terrible tricks on us when we are experiencing fear and confusion in our lives. And in that fear and confusion, they didn't recognise Jesus. But in the middle of this darkness, fear, and panic, Jesus says, 'It is I, be not afraid.' When you are in the middle of a storm, listen for His voice.

However, there is something that Jesus says which you might easily pass over, but it is so important. Jesus says, 'It is I.' The literal translation would be, 'It is *I am*.' Do you see what's happening here? The Name that God revealed for Himself to Moses at the burning bush was '*I am*.' Jesus is saying He is 'I am.' It is God. Don't be afraid.

Two chapters later, in John 8, Jesus says that before Abraham was, 'I am.' The Jews understood that Jesus was saying He was God, and they were about to stone Him. When the soldiers came to Gethsemane to arrest Jesus, and Jesus said, 'I am He,' the *'He'* is in italics. It wasn't in the original text but was inserted by the translators to make it read easier. When Jesus said, '*I am*,' the soldiers fell backward.

So, Jesus tells the disciples not to be afraid; it is 'I am'; it is God.

I wonder, is He saying that to you in your fear and panic in the middle of your storm today? Is He reminding you that He is the great 'I am'; therefore, don't be afraid, but rather, 'Be still, and know *I am* God'? (Psalm 46:10). He is the God of the wind and the seas and storms. You couldn't be in better hands.

DAY 79

Destination Guaranteed

Then they willingly received Him into the ship:
and immediately the ship was at the land where they went.
John 6:21

Why did Jesus perform this miracle of walking on the water? We all know that fishermen love to tell stories about the size of the fish they have caught. Was this miracle performed just so the disciples could tell another fisherman's story, only this time, they could tell how great a spectacle they saw? No, it was to demonstrate to them that Jesus is God and, not only that, but He is God of their storm.

Don't miss God in your storm. If, as a bonus, He performs a miracle in your storm, still, don't miss God in the miracle. Yes, He did that miracle to help you, but ultimately to show He is God. Matthew tells us they worshipped Him, and He wants us to bow down also in worship because He is God. Even if, in your storm, He doesn't perform a miracle (at least that you know of), yet, better than any miracle, is having Jesus in the boat with you and whispering peace to your soul.

John says that when Jesus got on the boat, immediately, the ship was on the other side. Even though they were only halfway over when the storm came (John tells us they had rowed 25 or 30 furlongs), suddenly, they are at the other side. Some think this was a miracle; a bit like Philip when he was taken by the Spirit and transported into the presence of the Ethiopian eunuch. That may or may not be the case. But one thing I know: if you have Jesus in your boat (that is, if you are saved), He will bring you safely to the other side. On a different occasion in Mark 4, Jesus said, 'Let us go over to the other side.' Despite the fierce storm that arose, they arrived safely on the other side. If Jesus declares that you are going to the other side (despite what satan throws at you) because He has spoken it, then your destination is guaranteed.

DAY 80

Counting The Cost

*For which of you, intending to build a tower, sits not down first,
and counts the cost, whether he have sufficient to finish it?*
Luke 14:28

We know the power of advertising. You can sit down after a busy day, with no intention of moving for the rest of the evening. Then you see an advert, and soon you are on your way to the local shop! From time to time, the army will advertise and, of course, they will try to attract those who not only wish to serve their country and to be involved in peace-keeping exercises, but also those who have a sense of adventure, adapt well to teamwork, and enjoy the camaraderie of army life. While these things may seem attractive to some, it would be unwise to take the matter any further until weighing up any negative aspects. How would you feel about potentially killing someone? Are you comfortable with discipline? Are you willing to keep in shape?

If we were to advertise about the Christian 'army', what would we include? '*Sign up today and get peace of mind,*' '*be forgiven,*' '*become a child of the King,*' '*know that you are going to Heaven when you die.*' All that sounds good, but sometimes we forget to tell people that there is a price to be paid. You see, while salvation is free, yet it will cost us everything as we lay our lives down before Jesus, and say, 'Be Lord of my life.' Sometimes we forget to tell people that Christians face problems just like anyone else. Everything does not suddenly become smooth and easy.

When we count the cost, we are tempted to weigh up the monetary cost. However, Jesus says to store up treasure in Heaven, rather than on earth (Matthew 6:19-21). As we count the cost, we need to weigh up time against eternity. Paul tells us in 2nd Corinthians 4:18 not to focus on the things that are temporal, but on those that are eternal. The bottom line is this: while you may lose out on some things while following Jesus, yet you will have gained everything that you will ever need as you serve Him. No-one ever loses out with Jesus.

DAY 81

Profit Or Loss?

For what shall it profit a man, if he shall gain the whole world, and lose his own soul? Or what shall a man give in exchange for his soul?
Mark 8:36,37

There's something satisfying about making a profit. Years ago, when car boot sales were gaining in popularity, I remember doing my first sale. Before I had even brought one item out, as soon as I opened the boot of the car, the potential buyers were trying to rummage through everything, like vultures around a body! But there was something satisfying about making some extra profit from things that, up until then, had just been lying around gathering dust. Jesus knows that profit and loss make us 'tick'. When He uses this language in today's verse, He looks at the highest stakes of all: the profit and loss of our soul; that precious eternal possession which each one of us has within.

There is a well-known story told about Alexander the Great. Here was a young man, a great military strategist, who conquered the known world of his day and the legend goes that, when he had conquered it all, he sat down and cried because he had no more worlds left to conquer. He literally had gained the whole world, and, still, he wasn't satisfied. He died at the age of 33, having conquered this world; but if he didn't know God, then he lost his soul. What a loss. By the way, they say that Jesus was around 33 when He was crucified, the same age that Alexander was when he died. At 33, Alexander had gained the world and lost his soul; while at 33, Jesus had died and His work on Calvary's cross was enough to save *the whole world,* if only they would believe. What a difference between these two deaths. There is something even more costly than the soul of man, and that is the price which Jesus paid on the cross to save our souls. That shows me how precious our souls are to God. That's the value God has put on our souls. No one needs to lose their soul because the price has been paid. It is the ultimate price, but it is left to each one of us to accept this free gift of salvation. Decide today!

DAY 82

Being Stretched

Knowing this, that the trying of your faith works patience.
James 1:3

Maybe as a parent you remember your child's first day at school, and you cried more than the child did. Or maybe you didn't. Maybe you couldn't wait to get them into school and run! But you left them with God that day and trusted Him to keep them. Perhaps it seemed like a small thing, but it was important to you. As life went on, and your child grew eventually into adulthood, your faith was stretched as they faced the different storms of life. Problems were much more complicated than that first day at school! But you trusted God to see them through. Our verse tells us that the trying of your faith produces patience (or endurance). Today, you are persevering and going through with God because your faith has been tested and stretched in the past, from the smaller things of life through to the bigger things.

Peter describes faith as being like gold; before it comes through in all its brilliance, it has to be tried in the fire (1st Peter 1:7). The dross (mineral waste or impurities) has to be removed and burned away before it can be called pure gold. No fire? No pure gold. Spiritually speaking, if there's no testing, you cannot be perfected in your faith. If your faith is in a healthy place today, it's because of the testing which you have gone through in the past.

It's like an athlete who is training for a 10k race. When they are training, they might start at 5k and then work their way up gradually to 10k. Their previous training gives them the ability to run the full race. And so it is with faith. Those difficult things you have come through are increasing your faith and stretching it, enabling you to believe for bigger things that you may not have been able to do a few years previous. Having our faith stretched is not comfortable, but it is needful. The result of this stretching (Peter goes on to say) is praise, honour and glory when Jesus comes again.

DAY 83

Trusting Without Seeing Immediate Results

When He had thus spoken, He spat on the ground, and made clay of the spittle, and He anointed the eyes of the blind man with the clay,
John 9:6

You talk about stretching your faith? This blind man who comes to Jesus for healing has had to put up with questions from the disciples about why he is blind. Jesus put the critics to silence, but now the man faces another obstacle to his faith. Jesus puts mud on his eyes and the blind man has to go and wash in the pool of Siloam to be healed. You can see how this man's faith is being stretched. Jesus didn't give him immediate healing, as He did in most other cases He dealt with. What was this man going to do in the intervening period? Was he going to just walk away? You remember Naaman almost walked away from his miracle because he didn't get healed the way he thought he was going to be healed. Jesus is asking this blind man to trust Him, even though he is walking around with clay on his eyes.

I wonder if that is your test or your trial today? You haven't received an immediate answer to your prayer, and in the intervening period, you are walking around (as it were) with clay on your eyes, and you cannot see the full picture. Also, other people have prayed for exactly the same thing as you have prayed for. They have received it, and you haven't (yet). The Lord seems to be working differently in your situation, and you don't understand why. This is the difficult part of faith, and it comes to each one of us. In those intervening periods when we have prayed but haven't received the answer, God is calling us to trust Him, even when we can't see the full picture and even when we don't understand.

The blind man obeys, though, and receives his sight in response to his faith. Hebrews 11:6 reminds us that God rewards faith. God doesn't always do things when we want, or how we want, but He always rewards faith. Keep trusting through the trial.

DAY 84

God Is Still On The Throne

*In the year that king Uzziah died I saw also the Lord sitting upon a
throne, high and lifted up, and His train filled the temple.*
Isaiah 6:1

A little boy came home from Sunday School. Later on, his
mum became a bit suspicious because he was very quiet!
When kids are quiet, something is going on! She found
him leafing through the phone book. She asked, 'What are you
doing son?' He replied, 'In Sunday School, we sang, "God is still
on the phone," and I'm looking for His phone number!' He had
mistaken the words of the chorus, 'God is still on the throne'!

King Uzziah was a great king who reigned for 52 years. On the
whole, he did that which was right before God. He was a great
military man, and a great builder; his fame spread throughout the
world of his day. However, his end was a sad one. Since he was
such a popular king, he forgot that God had blessed him and made
him great. He thought he was invincible and entered the temple of
God to offer incense on the altar (a thing that only the priests were
allowed to do). Even though the priests warned him and tried to
hold him back, he stubbornly went ahead and God struck him
down with leprosy. Isaiah, as a prophet of God, is no doubt
discouraged and heartbroken at how this great king could brazenly
defile the temple of God in such a way. At the moment of his great
discouragement, Isaiah gets a vision of the Lord sitting upon the
throne, in splendour. He learns the lesson that leaders come and
go, but the Lord always occupies His throne.

Sometimes, we look around our nation and see how it is in decline,
with God's laws being ignored. Just as the priests tried to restrain
Uzziah, so the church has spoken out on many issues, only at times
to be rejected by our Government. We become discouraged and
heartbroken. We need to do as Isaiah did and get a fresh vision of
the Lord today in all His majesty and glory. God is still on the
Throne. He always has been, and He always will be.

DAY 85

Dare To Be A Daniel

*Now when Daniel knew that the writing was signed, he went into his
house; and his windows being open in his chamber toward Jerusalem,
he kneeled upon his knees three times a day, and prayed,
and gave thanks before his God, as he did beforetime.*
Daniel 6:10

In the previous verse, we are told that King Darius signed the
decree that was going to ban Daniel and anyone like him from
praying to God for thirty days. There are times today also,
when governments sign laws that are contrary to the Word of God.

The easiest thing for Daniel would have been to say, '*Well, it's
only for thirty days. I will weather the storm for a month, and then
everything will be fine. No point losing my life over a decree for
thirty days.*' But Daniel stood strong. Even though many times
they may be in the minority, God always has His people, who will
stand strong upon the Word of God and not give in. Maybe you are
discouraged today and think that not many believe what you
believe. Elijah thought that too. He actually thought he was the
only one standing for God, but God informs him that He has seven
thousand who have not bowed the knee to Baal. Although general
opinion today is against what the Word of God teaches, don't be
discouraged. All over this world, God has His remnant, who are
still standing strong in faith.

The decree is passed, and what does Daniel do? He does what he
has always done. He opens his window and prays three times. The
law changed, *but it did not change Daniel!* It did not change his
devotion to his God. It was business as usual for Daniel, as far as
he and God were concerned. He was going to let nothing get in the
way between himself and God.

Keep standing strong in these difficult days. Laws may change, but
don't let them change you. Keep doing what you have always
done, and keep enjoying God's Presence. Dare to be a Daniel.

DAY 86

Limping Along

And as he passed over Penuel the sun rose upon him,
and he halted upon his thigh.
Genesis 32:31

One Tuesday night, the prayer meeting had just finished, and I got up to go to the door. As I stood up, I realised that whatever way I had been sitting, my leg had 'fallen asleep' and was numb. This put me in a predicament because I knew I had to walk in front of the congregation to go to the door. I started to limp across to the other side, trying unsuccessfully to hide it. I could hear some whispers in the background. I knew that once the people came outside, I was going to get a lot of questions: *'Are you OK? What happened?'* And when they heard what really happened, we had a bit of a laugh!

In the Bible, there was a man who, when you saw him walking along, did so with a limp. If someone had asked him, 'What's with the limp?' he would have had to tell them about a strange night when he wrestled with a mysterious being who put his thigh out of joint; but yet he still hung on for the blessing. That was a moment which he would never forget because his life had been changed, and even his name was changed. He went from *Jacob* (the deceiver) to *Israel*, (who had power with God). Jacob's limp told a story of pain, but also a story of surrender, followed by blessing.

In reality, if we want to go deeper with God, we will also walk with a limp. That limp is an indicator that we have pleaded with God for the blessing. He has broken us from our own stubborn will; we have surrendered all to Him and received the blessing. It is when we have been broken, that God can use us to the greatest potential. Paul said a strange thing in 2nd Corinthians 12:10. He said that when he is weak, then he is strong. Is Paul talking in riddles? No. It is when we are at our weakest that we seem to rely the most on God; and it is at times like these that His strength is made perfect in our weakness (see 2nd Corinthians 12:9).

DAY 87

Are You Satisfied?

For My people have committed two evils; they have forsaken Me
the fountain of living waters, and hewed them out cisterns,
broken cisterns, that can hold no water.
Jeremiah 2:13

One Saturday I went to my favourite fast food outlet and ordered a bargain bucket, consisting of ten pieces of chicken and four chips. (By the way, it wasn't all for me. I'm not that greedy!) When I got home and opened it up, there were ten pieces of chicken and zero chips. Some businesses do a survey for those who have used their services and they ask how satisfied you are with your experience in their shop. Usually, your answer is given using between one and five smiley faces. Well, for me that day, it wouldn't even have reached one smiley face. I wasn't happy at all! However, I normally get good service there.

Just as I was dissatisfied with the food, our verse today speaks about people who were disgruntled with what they had to drink spiritually. God's people had forsaken Him and made themselves spiritual cisterns to hold water. But these cisterns were broken. It would be like storing your water in a sieve. Totally useless.

If we forsake God and try to find satisfaction in anything else other than Himself, it is like storing water in a broken cistern. It may hold the water for a short time, but eventually disappears through the cracks. It doesn't last. Don't get me wrong; the world can be enjoyable, but there is a difference between enjoying something for a short time, and being permanently satisfied. This world's pleasures do not last. Solomon was a man who could enjoy whatever he wanted, totally unrestricted. All he had to do was ask for anything and he could have it. But in Ecclesiastes 1:2, Solomon gives his opinion of it all. He says, 'All is vanity.' This comes from the man who did it all, and who had it all, humanly speaking. You've heard it said before. Each person has a God-shaped vacuum in their heart that only He can fill. Let Him fill it today.

DAY 88

Rising Prices

Forasmuch as you know that you were not redeemed with corruptible things, as silver and gold, from your vain conversation received by tradition from your fathers; But with the precious blood of Christ, as of a lamb without blemish and without spot.
1st Peter 1:18-19

So, as you saw in the last message, I came home from the fast-food outlet and they had given me no chips. Well, I couldn't be bothered going all the way back and queueing up again, so I went to our local chippy down the road and bought chips there. When I went to pay, the lady who was serving me said, 'That will be £6.40.' It was that moment when £ signs '*kerching*' in your eyes. '£6.40? For two chips?' I looked it up online, and in 1980 you could get one fish supper for less than £1. Around that time, crisps were 10p, chocolate bars 14p, and a pint of milk 15p.

As I thought about rising prices, I was drawn to the fact that while this world's prices fluctuate (rising more than falling), yet, in what we call 'God's economy,' the 'prices' never change.

The price that man pays for sin will always remain the same. There is the same cost for sin today as there was all those ages ago when Adam first sinned. Romans 6:23 tells us that the ultimate price man pays for sin is death. Then there will always be the same price that needs to be paid *for* sin. Hebrews 9:22 reminds us that without the shedding of blood there is no forgiveness for sins.

Man today devalues the price of redemption by using cheap substitutes such as good works and church attendance; but 1st Peter 1 v 18-19 actually tells us that the ultimate price that was paid for man's redemption is so costly that the price far exceeds that of silver and gold. It is the precious Blood of Christ. No cheap substitutes can set you free; only the Blood of Jesus. Prices down here change, but 'God's economy' remains the same. We as God's people rejoice in the fact that the price has been paid in full for our sins and will never have to be paid again.

DAY 89

Abba Father

For you have not received the spirit of bondage again to fear;
but you have received the Spirit of adoption,
whereby we cry, Abba, Father.
Romans 8:15

One of the favourite places for little kids (and big kids too!) has got to be the zoo. Ellie has always been fascinated with elephants and Karis with giraffes. For me, it's the chimpanzee and Di loves the eagles. Did you ever come away from the zoo, though, with sadness because these amazing creatures are behind prison bars and not running free as God intended them to be? One of the saddest has got to be the eagle. This majestic bird that was made to soar up in the clouds has only a few metres of space in which it can fly. I would guess that, if you set it free, once it would soar up in the air where it was intended to be, it would never return to live behind prison bars.

We as God's people were made to soar free in the liberty with which Christ has set us free; and yet sometimes we return and get entangled with, as Paul calls it, the 'yoke of bondage' (Galatians 5:1). We return to prisons from which God has set us free.

Maybe it is old lifestyles, old sins, old habits. One prison that we often revisit, though, is the prison of fear. Paul reminds us in Romans 8 that we have not received the spirit of bondage *again* to fear, but the Spirit of adoption. He then adds, 'Whereby we cry Abba, Father.' Instead of going back to the prison of fear today, cry 'Abba, Father.'

What are you fearing? Tomorrow? *Abba, Father* holds tomorrow in His Hands. A battle you are facing? *Abba, Father* goes before you into battle and fights those battles for you. A person? If God (*Abba, Father*) be for us, who can be against us? A difficult situation in life? *Abba, Father* has promised that when you walk through the fire and flood, He will be with you. Place your yesterday, today, and tomorrow in the hands of *Abba, Father*.

DAY 90

Identifying Our Nineveh

Arise, go to Nineveh, that great city, and cry against it;
for their wickedness is come up before Me.
Jonah 1:2

It was just another typical school morning. The kids were slow to eat, as usual. After what seemed like the one-hundredth time telling Ellie to eat, it was at that point where I had to firmly raise my voice. 'Ellie; eat!' Karis leaned over to me and said, '*Daddy, shout louder at her!*' There's something with kids about seeing their siblings in trouble. Although they love them, they think it's funny to see them getting shouted at or punished!

That's kids. But what happens when it's an adult? God said to Jonah to go to Nineveh and preach to them. Jonah didn't want to go because he wanted to see them punished. A preacher who didn't want his listeners to repent! It's like a doctor who doesn't want his patients to get well. Why was this? Jonah had a touch of prejudice and even racism. The people of Nineveh were Gentiles; they were inferior. Israel were God's blessed people and he didn't want these mere Gentiles to be blessed by God.

I want to challenge each of us to search our hearts before the Lord. Is there a group of people or a person that, if God asked you to witness to them with the gospel, and do it with deep compassion, you couldn't do it with pure love in your heart for their souls? Maybe because of their skin colour, or maybe you couldn't witness because their religion is different from yours? Or maybe someone at work or in your family that you simply do not like?

Whoever it is that you have thought of, guess what? You have just identified your own personal '*Nineveh*!' In response, don't buy a ticket to Tarshish. You know how that turns out! I believe God wants to deal with our hearts, just as He did with Jonah. Let's not be reluctant spreaders of God's Word; but let us follow God's leading and go to our Nineveh with hearts full of love and compassion.

DAY 91

The Two Handles Of Tomorrow

Which of you by taking thought can add one cubit to his stature?
Matthew 6:27

I remember well the time when Di was learning to drive (I want to emphasise that she was good, or I will be in trouble!). As I was sitting in the passenger seat, the cars seemed very close. I kept thinking she was going to hit nearby wing mirrors (which she never did). But was I worried? Yes. Did I totally trust that she was in control? I'll be honest, no. Even though she was! Sometimes I felt like grabbing the steering wheel, not because she was a bad driver, but because I was worried. In a similar way, worry implies that God is not powerful enough to deal with what is going on in our lives. Are we able to allow God to be the driver in our lives? Do we try to grab the steering wheel sometimes?

I don't need to tell you that worry doesn't change anything. In our verse, Jesus says that you can't add anything to your height by worrying. Worrying just makes your mind tired and eats away at your joy. Someone has said that worry is like a rocking chair. It gives you plenty to do, but you never get anywhere with it! Most of us cannot remember what it was we were worried about this day five years, ten years, or twenty years ago.

However, while many of the things we worry about never actually happen, some things we worry about *do* come to pass. Maybe some sort of bad news, a health issue, or financial concern; but even then, worry cannot change the situation. You have probably heard it said that *worry* is a conversation you have with yourself about things you cannot change. But *prayer* is a conversation you have with God about things *He can change*. Bring your anxieties to Jesus.

Henry Ward Beecher said that every tomorrow is like a door. It has two handles. We can take hold of it with the handle of *worry*, or the handle of *faith*. May God give us all grace to choose faith.

DAY 92

A Look At Ourselves

And he laid it upon my mouth, and said, Lo, this has touched your lips; and your iniquity is taken away, and your sin purged.
Isaiah 6:7

In Isaiah 6, the prophet got a view of God's holiness. When that happens, the natural reaction should be to see the contrast of our own sinfulness. Isaiah cries out, 'Woe is me, for I am undone.' He's saying, '*I'm doomed. There's no hope. It's all over.*' Notice Isaiah said, 'Woe is *me*, for I am undone.' He didn't say, '*Wait a minute Lord, You should let wee Jimmy next door see this vision of Yourself; he needs it; he's a real bad sinner*!'

I was doing door-to-door evangelism with some others. A man came to the door and we talked for a while. He said, 'You should go to that house over there; he's in a bad way; he's an alcoholic.' And then he used a phrase that I will never forget. He added that the man was 'past redemption.' Wow. I thought that was a big statement. So, I said to the man, 'What about yourself? Are you saved?' Guess what? He said no. Yet he was telling me to go across the road to somebody he thought needed it more than him! And yet they both needed it equally.

Thank God, though, Isaiah not only got a look at the Lord and a look at himself, but he got a look at an altar. Obviously, Isaiah could see the altar, as he watched the seraphim take the coal off the altar and apply it to his lips. The seraphim says that Isaiah's iniquity is taken away and his sin is purged. The altar made the difference. Jesus' sacrifice makes the difference for us also.

Jesus tells of the Pharisee and the tax collector who came before God. The Pharisee thinks that this old tax collector needs help, but that he himself is *OK*. He didn't get a proper look at himself in relation to God. It was the tax collector, who cried out, 'God be merciful to me, a sinner,' that received the blessing. It's not an easy thing for us to see ourselves as God sees us. But when we do, we are on the road to blessing.

DAY 93

Fire-Watchers

And the angel of the LORD appeared to him in a flame of fire out of the midst of a bush: and he looked, and, behold, the bush burned with fire, and the bush was not consumed.
Exodus 3:2

Isn't it funny how people are attracted to fire? They just *must* have a look! I remember during the '*Troubles*' in Northern Ireland, there were a few bombs over the years in the town centre in which we lived. There would be a chilling silence just after you heard a bomb go off. The normal thing to do is keep away from trouble, but some people would come out of their houses, make their way into town towards the bomb, and towards the fire! They usually did it for one of two reasons. Some went down simply because they were nosey! But a very small minority went to ransack the shops where the glass had blown in.

People then, for some reason, are attracted to fire. John Wesley said to get 'on fire' for God and others will come to watch you 'burn'. When a church or a person is 'on fire' for God, word spreads, and people observe that there is something supernatural happening. It stands out from the normal. Too many people have come into contact with dead religion; they are put off by it, and you can't blame them. If all the world observes is dead religion, then it is hard for them to see the living Christ in all of that. They wrongly conclude that our Saviour is unapproachable and cold, and that serving Him must be dull and boring because that has been their experience with dead religion.

The world needs to come into contact with a vibrant, living church, alive with love for Christ, alive with the gospel, alive with love for each other, alive with the freedom of the Holy Spirit, and alive with compassion for a lost world. Alive, and wanting to see others being filled with life. May we be like the burning bush that Moses encountered and keep on 'burning' for God!

DAY 94

Don't Give Up On Revival

Will they revive the stones out of the heaps
of the rubbish which are burned?
Nehemiah 4:2

I have heard of spiritual revival being described simply as, 'When God comes down.' There was revival when Jesus came *down* from Heaven, preaching, teaching, healing, and bringing life through what He did at Calvary. There was revival when the Holy Spirit was sent *down* on the day of Pentecost.

Leonard Ravenhill said, 'In revival, God is not concerned about filling empty churches, He is concerned about filling empty hearts.' Vance Havner said that revival 'Is the church falling in love with Jesus Christ all over again.'

Revival is usually preceded by a thirsting and a hungering for God, which is accompanied by intensified prayer. There also is a great sense of fear and reverence towards God, alongside a desire for holiness and obedience to the Lord. The Word of God takes a prominent place among God's people and becomes alive in their hearts.

Some say that the times we live in are too dark for revival, yet some of the greatest revivals came in the darkest of days. Apart from that, revival is not dependent upon what is going on in the world at the time, it is more dependent upon what is going on with God's people. Revival comes when His people, who are called by His Name, humble themselves, pray, seek His face, and turn from their wicked ways (see 2nd Chronicles 7:14).

There will always be those who say it's no use to pray for revival; *'It isn't coming, so just give up. People have been chasing that for years.'* The people of Nehemiah's day faced that challenge. In Nehemiah 4, as they began to rebuild the wall, they were mocked. *'Can they revive the stones out of heaps of rubbish?'* But they prayed, kept on building, and revival came. Don't give up on revival.

DAY 95

Wet Feet!

He that believes on Me, as the scripture has said, out of his belly shall flow rivers of living water. (But this spoke He of the Spirit, which they that believe on Him should receive: for the Holy Ghost was not yet given; because that Jesus was not yet glorified.)
John 7:38-39

Jesus speaks of those who believe in Him; and then He adds, 'As the Scripture has said.' So, this is Scriptural, and has Jesus' seal upon it. What will happen? 'Out of his belly shall flow rivers of living water.' Just in case anyone is in any doubt as to what this means, John helpfully adds that Jesus was speaking of the Spirit, which they that believe on Him should receive.

You can see the superabundance of what Jesus is talking about. It's not a trickle of water from a dripping tap; it's rivers of living water. Not the still waters of Psalm 23, but rather of great power. Jesus said these rivers will flow from anyone who believes in Him. You cannot hide forceful rivers. In the book of Acts, we see the effects of those rivers, as the church touches this world for Jesus.

These rivers today come from the same source as back then. This is the same Spirit in operation today, as He was back then. The writer to the Hebrews proclaims that Jesus Christ is the same yesterday, today, and forever. There's a river of life flowing in you and me, the power of the Holy Spirit; and there is an unending supply of these rivers of waters; there's as much as we will ever want in this lifetime, and eternity to come. Many are queueing up to get filled with other things in this life, but God's people should be marked by the fact that they are queueing up to get filled, refilled, and overflowing with these rivers of living water.

When we are filled to overflowing, it will become obvious. I think it's an old proverb from another country which says that you know your bucket of water is filled to overflowing when your feet are wet! Lord, fill us to overflowing, and may our spiritual feet be soaked with the rivers of living water!

DAY 96

Singing In The Storm

I will bless the Lord at all times:
His praise shall continually be in my mouth.
Psalm 34:1

The title above this Psalm in the Bible informs us that it is a Psalm of David, when he changed his behaviour before Abimelech. David was at one of the lowest points of his life up until this time and was on the run from Saul. He had left behind his best friend, Jonathan, and had no food or weapons. David then went to Gath and tried to seek sanctuary, but the people were suspicious of him and he feared for his life. David then pretended to be mad. He made scratches on the doors of the gate, and let his spittle run down his beard. They quickly got rid of him and he escaped to the wilderness. He then entered a cave, known as Adullam. Things could not have been much worse for David.

Maybe, like David, you have succumbed to doubts and fears over situations in your life. But I want to remind you that the mighty David, the one who killed a bear and a lion with his own hands, who slew Goliath, and who heard the song in his ears, 'Saul has slain his thousands, but David his tens of thousands;' this same David, one day pretended to be mad. If it can happen to David, well, at least we know that even great men of faith have feared, and that gives us some hope. But how sad to see this mighty man with the spittle running down his beard. The scary thing is that he did it so well everyone believed him! You see, no child of God is a 'super-saint', whatever that might be! We all are human. We all have succumbed to fear. We all need God's power.

Would you take the time to read this whole Psalm today? It is a Psalm of deliverance. The lesson we learn here is that, even though David, through fear, temporarily took his eyes off the Lord, yet God in His mercy delivered him. The first ten verses are really a song. David is singing at one of the lowest points of his life! Only God can give a song in a fearful place. He can do it for you too.

DAY 97

Get In The Cave!

David therefore departed from there, and escaped to the cave Adullam:
and when his brethren and all his father's house heard it,
they went down there to him.
1st Samuel 22:1

We saw yesterday that David had been temporarily out of the will of God. He had been on the run and, being afraid, he went to the land of the Philistines. They were suspicious of his motives. David felt endangered and pretended to be mad. He ended up in a cave all alone. However, there were a few amazing things that happened when David was in this cave. When his family heard he was there, they came and were reunited with David. Then we read that later, 400 men joined themselves to David and he became captain over them. God turns a grand total of one person in a cave into 401, plus his family. What do we learn from this? Whatever it is in your life that you are concerned about, never lose sight of the fact that it is God Who gives the increase. Look to Him.

David then goes to Moab and has a chat with the prophet, Gad. He is seeking God's Will again at last. Gad tells David not to stay in the cave but to go to the *land of Judah*. David obeys. Do you know where David originally had been on the run from? The *land of Judah!* David was being sent back to the very place from which he had escaped. Just as Jonah ended up in Nineveh, the place from which he also had been on the run. God has a way of getting us back into the place He wants us to be, but sometimes He has to get our attention. For Jonah, it was a whale, and for David, it was a cave. The great thing is that David returns to the land of Judah as a different man from when he left. He is now back in God's will.

I wonder if we have wandered out of God's will? Get alone with God in the cave. He wants to realign us with what He desires for our lives. The cave can be a lonely place at times, but it is often the place where the fire of our hearts is reignited.

DAY 98

God's Masterpiece

For we are His workmanship, created in Christ Jesus to good works,
which God has before ordained that we should walk in them.
Ephesians 2:10

When we were young, most of our toys were marked with the words, '*Made in China.*' Someone has said that if there was a stamp put on a Christian, it would say, '*Made in Heaven!*' You are God's very own workmanship (or handiwork). The word here for workmanship in the original Greek is '*poeima*'. Guess what word we get from that? Our word, poem. Yes, you are God's poem; His work of poetry. This word can also be translated as 'work of art'. What God is making out of you is a work of art, a masterpiece. Turn round to a spouse or a loved one as you are reading this. Tell them they are a work of art, and watch them fall off the chair in shock! Maybe you look at yourself and you say, '*I'm no masterpiece.*' That is true. None of us are – yet.

A while back we got a small pottery kit for the kids. When we used it, we found that we definitely didn't get it right on the first go; or the second; or the third. In fact, I don't think we got it 'right' at all. The process took a lot of care, a steady hand, and the right amount of water. We didn't declare our work 'finished' halfway through the process, but only after we had moulded, shaped, and sometimes started over again. No, we aren't masterpieces yet, although we *are* in God's eyes because He sees us '*in Jesus*'. The Lord still has some work to do. He has to add a few things, rub some things out, and lovingly mould us.

Imagine if you could commission anyone from history to paint a masterpiece for you. Who would you choose? Van Gough? Monet? Michelangelo? I'm impressed, but not as impressed as when I think of Who is making a masterpiece out of you and me: the One Who made this beautiful world. What a track record. The finished product? Made in the image of our Lord Jesus Christ. *Wow!*

DAY 99

Taken Away!

*For then must He often have suffered since the foundation of the world:
but now once in the end of the world has He appeared
to put away sin by the sacrifice of Himself.*
Hebrews 9:26

The thing about the Old Testament sacrifices was that the priests' work was never done. Hebrews 10:11 says that the priests stood daily, offering sacrifices that could never take away sins. There was no end to this sacrificial system. It just went on and on, not only for the priest but for the people. Each person knew that they were going to have to keep on coming to this place of sacrifice because, as these sacrifices could not take away sin, it meant that they only *covered* sin.

When I was a boy, I had some sort of fascination for numbers. Apparently, I memorised phone numbers from our family phone book and wrote the numbers on the wallpaper in my bedroom! Now, if it were possible (but I was too young), I could have got some furniture and put it in front of the numbers to hide the mess; when Mum would come into the room, the numbers might be covered, but I would still *know* in my heart they were there. But imagine Mum got someone to remove the old wallpaper, put on new wallpaper, and forgave me (which she eventually did!), then the numbers are not only covered but they are *completely taken away*.

Hebrews 9:26 says, 'Now once in the end of the world has He appeared to put away sin by the sacrifice of Himself.' On the cross, Jesus didn't just cover our sins, but He *took them away*! No more priests are needed to stand daily making sacrifices that could never take away sins, but Jesus offered a once-and-for-all sacrifice for sins. John 19:30 tells us that the work is finished. All that needed to be done has been done. Your sins are not just covered; they have been taken away, never to be held against you ever again. No one can uncover your sins because they aren't there to uncover!

DAY 100

Smiling At The Storm

And He said to them, Why are you so fearful?
how is it that you have no faith?
Mark 4:40

What's that kids' chorus? 'With Christ in the vessel, we can smile at the storm, as we go sailing home.' The disciples are in a boat with Jesus, a storm is raging, and they *ain't smilin'* at the storm! They are fearful. And fear makes you do some silly things! They wait until the boat has filled up with water before they wake Jesus! Isn't it strange how so often we make prayer our last-minute desperate call after we have exhausted every other option? But at least they eventually call on Jesus and He calms the storm.

So why were the disciples not smiling at the storm as they went sailing home? Jesus was in the vessel with them, but they were scared out of their wits. You see, the Presence of Jesus with us *should* bring us peace in the storm, but it depends on what we do with His Presence. We can either rest in His Presence or hang onto our fears.

Here's a wee contrast. The disciples in the boat, with Jesus in their midst, feared. The Psalmist, in the valley of the shadow of death, said, 'You are with me,' and therefore he would fear no evil. They both reacted differently to the Presence of Jesus in their storm! How are we reacting to His Presence? It's not only the Presence of Jesus *with* us that is important, but we also have to *lay our fears to rest* in His Presence. Then we can enjoy calm in His Presence.

I wonder, do we need to do that today? We know that Jesus has promised to never leave us nor forsake us; but have we laid our fears to rest in His Presence, or are we fearing, even though He is in the boat with us? How will we finish this chorus today? *'With Christ in the vessel I will'* - what? Is it *smile at the storm*? Or is it *fear the storm*? It's not easy. We are human. But may the Lord help each one of us to lay our fears to rest in His Presence.

DAY 101

The Grass Is Always Greener

For I was envious at the foolish, when I saw the prosperity of the wicked.
Psalm 73:3

The grass is always greener on the other side. Of course it is! When things are going badly, then everyone else's life seems so much more attractive. Just like the car comparison websites, so often we live our lives comparing ourselves to other people. We try to keep up with the Joneses. All this, of course, can unsettle our minds and make us envious of others. It can become even more dangerous when we do it in the spiritual realm. In times of difficulty, have you ever looked at the unsaved and it seems that they are having a great time? In Psalm 73, the Psalmist was becoming envious as he watched the wicked.

But, of course, all is not as it seems. Do you think the unsaved are happy within their hearts? Let me bring you behind the closed doors of the unsaved and take a peek behind the outer veneer. Isaiah 57:20-21 reminds us that those without God are like the troubled sea which rises and falls; they have no rest or peace. Instead of looking at the ungodly and envying them, we should take three looks elsewhere.

Look at their final destination: in Psalm 73, the Psalmist sees the true end of the ungodly and it is destruction.

Look to Jesus: fix your eyes on Him, the true source of peace and happiness.

Look at your own grass: does the grass seem greener on the other side because we are neglecting our own garden?

Tend to your own grass and garden. Clear up the weeds with the truth of the Word of God. Let the rays of the sunshine of intimacy with God help you to grow that which is good. Let the rain of the Spirit bring lushness and vibrancy, showing the beauty of Jesus; so much so that, instead of you envying the garden of the ungodly, they start to desire a garden like yours!

DAY 102

Intensified Anticipation

Not forsaking the assembling of ourselves together, as the manner of
some is; but exhorting one another: and so much the more,
as you see the day approaching.
Hebrews 10:25

How many times have I heard the words, 'Daddy, how many more sleeps until…?' Especially around Christmas. The kids ask about three months beforehand and it's scary how quickly ninety sleeps become just one. Maybe I'm just getting older. Then comes the final night, Christmas Eve. Oh, the anticipation; oh, the excitement; oh, the tension. Oh, the sleeplessness! As they have been counting down for the last three months now, they are so hyped up, they can't sleep. We inadvertently solved this problem one year when Di had to work on Christmas Day. To avoid her missing the kids opening their presents, we treated Christmas Eve as Christmas Day. They slept like a log the night before because they still thought there was one more sleep to go. That was accidental genius!

There's something about anticipation. The writer to the Hebrews is talking about an approaching Day which should cause anticipation and longing. It is the Day of Jesus' Return. How do we know it is approaching? Well, how do you know that the day of a baby's birth is fast approaching? A word called '*contractions*'. They start and stop, and start and stop, getting closer as the moment of birth nears. Jesus said that as His Return approaches, the signs of the times will increase, just like contractions before childbirth.

What should we do as the Day approaches? We shouldn't fear, but rather, as our verse says, we should not forsake the assembling of ourselves together. We ought to meet together regularly with the aim of encouraging each other in the Lord. In fact, it says to do it even more as that Day approaches. As the nearness of that Day intensifies, our encouragement of one another should intensify. Are we excited? Are we anticipating? Jesus is coming soon!

DAY 103

Ask Big

Now to Him that is able to do exceeding abundantly above all that we ask or think, according to the power that works in us,
Ephesians 3:20

Granny McKinley was widowed at a relatively young age and had to bring up my mother in the early 1950s. Imagine what a struggle that was for a single parent, especially in the days after World War 2. Her brother-in-law had emigrated some years before to the USA and had done very well for himself. He came over one year for a visit. As mum was his brother's only child, he was very fond of her, and she of him. Out of the blue, he said to his young niece, 'Lorna, if there's anything your little heart desires, ask me for it and I will give it to you.' Granny was horrified. What would mum ask for? Would she embarrass her with a request that was too big? Would she embarrass her brother-in-law? All eyes turned to mum, and she said, 'I would love a chip (*French fries*) in a paper!' Granny exhaled a sigh of relief!

When we ask God for things in prayer, we can never embarrass Him. Nothing is too big for God. He is able to do immeasurably more than we can ask or think. Nothing is impossible with Him. Sometimes we think we shouldn't bring our small problems to the Almighty either, yet He is concerned with the fall of the sparrow, and cares about the seemingly insignificant things in our lives.

When you pray, whether it is a small or a big matter, *pray big*. Don't limit God. James reminds us that we don't have some things because we don't ask for them. That doesn't mean if you ask for a jumbo jet, you will get one. But when I say ask big, I'm not talking about greed. I mean don't put God 'in a box'. Do you think your prodigal will never return? Do you think that problem in work or at home will never change? Ask big. What *you* think God is capable of doing is only a drop in the ocean compared to what He *really* is able to do!

DAY 104

One Day At A Time

Give us this day our daily bread.
Matthew 6:11

Many years ago, my mum's uncle Theo (whom I mentioned in yesterday's devotion) came over from America to stay for a holiday on a separate occasion, when mum was older. One morning he asked, 'Lorna, where's the milk?' She replied, 'In the fridge.' He said, 'Where's the fridge? I don't see it.' She said, 'Open the back door.' He opened the door and the milk was sitting in a bucket of cold water. That was the fridge! He was a very generous man though and it wasn't long until mum had her first fridge.

In Bible times, of course, there were no fridges. This prayer petitions God to 'Give us this day our daily bread,' and it was literally a day-to-day supply they needed as it wasn't just as easy to preserve food in those times.

When God's people were in the wilderness for forty years, God performed a miracle. In a desert, He sent them bread from Heaven to eat. Faithfully, every day, it was there. They didn't appreciate this miracle and began to grumble. Imagine grumbling about a miracle! They became *familiar* with God's supernatural acts. May we never become familiar with the things of God.

Just as they had to depend on God one day at a time, so this prayer is a prayer of total dependence upon God, one day at a time. As with the physical, so with the spiritual. Man cannot live by bread alone, but by every Word that proceeds from the mouth of God (Matthew 4:4). Spiritually speaking, do we have a balanced diet? Are we spiritually starving? If we were to get a spiritual x-ray of our soul, would it be all skin and bones? Are we being nourished?

We need the true Bread Who came down from Heaven - Jesus. We are totally dependent upon Him and we need Him on a day-by-day basis. We can have a daily spiritual banquet as we feast with Jesus. One day at a time.

DAY 105

Radical Forgiveness

Then said Jesus, Father, forgive them; for they know not what they do.
And they parted His raiment, and cast lots.
Luke 23:34

Sometimes we may try to wriggle out of forgiving others by using the excuse that they haven't said '*sorry*'. The greatest example of forgiveness was when Jesus was dying on the cross. Those responsible had treated Him in the most barbaric and cruel way imaginable. As He hung there, bleeding and dying, Jesus prayed, 'Father, forgive them, for they know not what they do.' One thief asked for forgiveness but that was about it. None of the crowd asked for forgiveness. None of the soldiers asked for forgiveness (except perhaps the centurion, who recognised that Jesus was the Son of God). The Jewish leaders never asked for forgiveness. Jesus still prayed for them.

Let's look at one of Jesus' followers: Stephen. As he was being stoned to death, he looked at those who were murdering him and knelt down, crying out with a loud voice, 'Father, lay not this sin to their charge.' None of them asked for forgiveness, but Stephen forgave them. Stephen was being a true disciple of Jesus by following in his Master's footsteps in regard to forgiveness. As followers of Jesus, we also will need to forgive those who do not ask for forgiveness. Jesus taught us to love our enemies and to bless those who curse us. Jesus did that on the cross and Stephen did that as the stones were flying at him.

God knows how we are wired up. He should. He made us! And as our Creator and Father, He wants what is best for us, just as we would want what is best for our kids. He knows that when we forgive (despite the person not having asked for forgiveness), this helps to keep us from being chained in our minds by bitterness and coldness (which can even be the cause of making us physically and emotionally sick). Is there anyone we need to forgive? Let us follow the Master in His example. This is radical forgiveness. It's not easy, but it's the right thing to do. Ask His Spirit to help us.

DAY 106

Well-Balanced Study

These were more noble than those in Thessalonica, in that they received the word with all readiness of mind, and searched the scriptures daily, whether those things were so.
Acts 17:11

I was flying to England for a conference and when I got to the plane, it wasn't one of the big jumbo jets, but a smaller one with propellers. When I boarded the plane, I heard the flight attendant asking someone from the front to move to the back. And then she asked if anyone else would be willing to move back. I was astounded to find out that the reason for this was to balance out the plane. There were too many passengers at the front. The thought of having to balance out a plane made me feel uneasy. It may have been a good idea to start reciting the 23rd Psalm!

When it comes to false teaching, the best way we can guard against it is a *well-balanced* study of the Scriptures. Mere superficial knowledge of the Bible is not sufficient. Some years ago, a plane crashed over Germany killing many because a radar tower was not properly monitoring the air traffic. When our spiritual radar isn't functioning, we will be deceived, and disaster can come.

In Acts 17, the Bereans searched the Scriptures daily to see if what Paul was telling them matched up with the Word of God. Their radars were on. The late Chuck Missler used to say, 'Don't believe anything I tell you; go home and check the Scriptures!' Of course, he wasn't insinuating that he was dishonest, but using humour to make a point. The point is that we need to be people of *'the Book'*.

False teachers both look and sound plausible. Many times, they can have great personalities and possess an amazing way with words. Those who don't know the Word of God well enough are easy prey for these wolves in sheep's clothing. When you know the Word of God, you will sniff out false teaching from miles away. There will be something in your spirit discerning that it's not right. Be a Berean. Have a well-balanced approach to studying God's Word.

DAY 107

A Finished Work

When Jesus therefore had received the vinegar, He said, It is finished:
and He bowed His head, and gave up the ghost.
John 19:30

You cannot add to a finished work. I painted our fence last year, all the way around the back and the front. It was hard work. Before I make myself sound too heroic, it hadn't been painted for a few years. That painted fence was a combined team effort of my hard labour and Di's continual 'encouragement' to get it done! But if I had put the last brush-stroke of paint on it, declared it finished, and then returned five minutes later to paint some more, what would that tell you? It wasn't really finished. It's not finished until you put down all your work tools and don't touch it anymore. If you have to add to it, then it's not finished.

When Jesus cried out on the cross, 'It Is Finished,' He meant what He said. If anyone tries to add to what Jesus did at Calvary, then that means it wasn't finished and we know that cannot be true. It's Jesus plus nothing. No additions. Paul explains in Colossians 2:14-15 why nothing else is necessary. All that the law had charged us with was blotted out through Jesus' death. One minute the writing against us was there and the next minute it was gone.

One day, when we were out with the kids, we saw a guy doing some tricks. He had a painting book with drawings (which had no colours), leafed through it, and then suddenly it was full of colours. He leafed through it again and now, not only the colours, but also the drawings had completely disappeared. It was totally blank. What he did was a simple trick, but what happened at Calvary was *no trick*. Just like the book that once was full of drawings (until they suddenly disappeared), so the book that contained the charges against us through the law is now totally blank because of Calvary. You can search through that book from now to eternity and find no charges whatsoever. Praise God, my sins are gone!

DAY 108

Turning The Bitter To Sweet

And when they came to Marah, they could not drink of the waters of Marah, for they were bitter: therefore, the name of it was called Marah.
Exodus 15:23

We read here that Moses and the people came to Marah, where the waters were bitter. We all come to *Marah* in our lives, but it's what we do when we get there that makes the difference. Naomi, when she lost her husband and sons, changed her name to *Mara,* meaning bitter. It is a slightly different spelling but the same meaning. She said that she went out full, but came back empty and the Lord had afflicted her. While of course we can sympathise with Naomi and understand her asking the question '*why?*' (the Psalmist many times asks the question '*why?*'), yet she is going further than that. She has become bitter against the Lord. This bitterness is eating her up. God's mercy later on turned her bitterness back to sweetness; but had it not been for that, Naomi was on the road to becoming a bitter old woman.

On the other hand, Job loses not only ten children, but his cattle and his possessions. This made his wife bitter and she said to Job, 'Curse God and die.' However, we read that in all that happened, Job didn't sin, or charge God foolishly. What a testimony! The blind writer Fanny Crosby had every reason to be bitter, as it seems that a 'quack' doctor was responsible for her blindness shortly after her birth. Her father also died soon after this incident. She could have played that over and over in her mind all her life, but she went on to write eight thousand hymns to the glory of God.

Most people refer to this passage as, '*the bitter waters of Marah.*' But there is every reason to call it '*the sweet waters of Marah*' because God intervened in the situation and caused the waters to become sweet. Today, you may be going through a bitter experience in your life. Through His grace, it is possible one day to look back at what you thought was bitter and watch how God made something sweet out of it.

DAY 109

The Right Perspective

*For where two or three are gathered together in My name,
there am I in the midst of them.*
Matthew 18:20

D o you ever find your mind wandering in church? *'I
wonder, did I remember to switch on the oven before I
left?' 'Why is he sitting beside her today? I never would
have put those two together.' 'Why did Jimmy not look at me this
morning when I went to say hello?'*

We are there in the body, but our mind has left the building! We
are *there.* We've clocked in and done our part, but we are so
distracted and our minds are wandering.

*'If they sing that song again....' 'If they don't sing that song the
way I like it....' 'If the pastor preaches on that subject again, I'm
just going to switch off.'* When something displeases us in church,
we disconnect. We get fixated on something, and week after week
that fixation gets a hold of us, and it steals our focus and attention
from Jesus.

We have the wrong perspective of church when it becomes about
anything else other than Jesus Christ. As Rutherford/Cousin wrote,
'The bride eyes not her garment, but her dear bridegroom's face.'
When we come and meet together, we are the bride coming to gaze
on the Bridegroom. Paul says, 'That in all things He might have
the pre-eminence' (Colossians 1:18).

Jesus is the main attraction; in fact, He is the *only* attraction when
we meet together. Today's verse says that He is in the midst. Is He
really? Or what do we have at the centre of our attention when we
come to meet together? Don't miss out on His Presence the next
time you go to church. Don't miss out on His centrality. Don't
miss out on His Pre-eminence. He awaits to show us great and
wonderful things if we don't allow ourselves to get distracted.
'Lord, help us to see You today.'

DAY 110

Scapegoat

And Aaron shall cast lots upon the two goats;
one lot for the LORD, and the other lot for the scapegoat.
Leviticus 16:8

Many of you may remember the 1994 World Cup in the USA. Colombia was playing against the host nation. One of their players was called Andrés Escobar (nicknamed 'the gentleman' because of his good nature) and he accidentally scored an own goal. All Colombia needed was a draw with the USA to make the next round but, due to this unfortunate accident, they went out of the competition. A few weeks later, back in Colombia, Escobar was shot six times in a car park by three men. They were part of a drug cartel and had set themselves up as both judge and jury, making Escobar the scapegoat for Colombia's World Cup exit.

The scapegoat concept goes all the way back to Leviticus 16 and a Jewish Holy Day called the Day of Atonement (known as Yom Kippur). The High Priest was to take two goats. One was to be 'for the Lord' and was to be sacrificed. The blood was sprinkled on the mercy seat on the Ark of the Covenant.

Then the High Priest came to the second goat, the scapegoat. He laid his hands on its head and confessed the sins of the people over it, reminding us of the amazing words from Isaiah 53:6, 'And the LORD has laid on Him the iniquity of us all.' The goat would then be led through the crowd and far away into the wilderness, into a forgotten place. That's exactly what happens when our sins, having been laid on Jesus, are carried far away, never to be remembered against us anymore. Psalm 103:12 says, 'As far as the east is from the west, so far has He removed our transgressions from us.'

A scapegoat often is one person who takes the blame for a group of people. What an amazing thought that Jesus took the blame and the punishment for all our sins. And not only that; He removes them to where they can never be brought up again. What a Saviour!

DAY 111

The Last Word

Now it came to pass in the days when the judges ruled, that there was a famine in the land. And a certain man of Bethlehem-Judah went to sojourn in the country of Moab, he, and his wife, and his two sons.
Ruth 1:1

The Bible is a love story from Genesis to Revelation and the book of Ruth is a love story contained within this bigger love story. The opening words of a book can be the difference between you reading the rest of the story or just setting it aside. Who will confess to leafing over to the end of a book and reading the closing words to see how it all ends?

The opening words of Ruth give minimal background to the story. We read, 'Now it came to pass,' and are told of a journey that a family makes away from their home, to the land of Moab. By verse 3 the husband is dead, and by verse 5, the two sons are dead. What a dramatic opening! If you were to write the story of your own life, beginning with '*Now it came to pass,*' I wonder what dramatic things have happened to you? Some good and some bad. We all have a story to tell, and each day a new chapter is being added.

However, the final words of the book of Ruth are absolutely amazing, and yet you could almost miss their importance and read quickly over them. The book ends in the most unexciting way (at least to the casual reader). It ends with a genealogy! I mean, what way is that to end a book? Besides, you usually put the genealogy at the start! But the very last verse tells us that Obed was Jesse's father, and then Jesse was David's father. In this story that begins with hopelessness and ends with hope, Ruth becomes the great-grandmother of King David, through whose family line (humanly speaking) the Messiah will come. David hasn't been born yet, but this coming king gets the last word in Ruth's story. If you are a Christian, no matter what has 'come to pass' in the story of your life, I want to remind you that, no matter what your circumstances are, the coming King (Jesus) gets the last word in your story too!

DAY 112

'Hesed' On Your Head And Heels

Who redeems your life from destruction;
who crowns you with lovingkindness and tender mercies;
Psalm 103:4

There is a Hebrew word that you need to know and to understand because it will help you through the worst times of life. It is used repeatedly in the Old Testament and is so important. It is the word *'hesed'*. It describes faithful, unfailing love and kindness. The reason why this word should be of great interest to us is because it describes the very character of our God.

Monarchs wear an expensive and glittering crown on their head that everyone can gaze at. Did you know that you wear a more valuable crown than any monarch? Nobody sees it, but it is there just the same. Psalm 103:4 tells us that God *crowns us* with lovingkindness. That is the word *hesed*. Pause, and let that truth filter through your heart and mind for a moment. Wherever you go today, you are crowned with God's faithful and unfailing love. Not only are you crowned with this *hesed*, but did you know it is following your every step? In Psalm 23:6, we read about goodness and mercy following us all the days of our lives. You have probably heard goodness and mercy being described as the Shepherd's sheep dogs that follow relentlessly after His people. The Hebrew word for mercy in Psalm 23:6 is, again, *hesed*. Wherever you go, whatever you do, God's faithful and unfailing love and kindness are pursuing you. Maybe you don't feel it, maybe you don't see it, but it is true because His Word says so.

Naomi had reached *Ground Zero*. She had lost her husband and two sons. She changed her name to 'bitter' and thought God had forgotten her. One day, Ruth came home from the fields of Boaz with stories about the great grace that he had shown to her. Noami's heart filled with hope, and she called out a blessing on Boaz from the Lord Whose kindness (*hesed*) had not ceased. Whatever you are facing today, don't lose hope. God's *hesed* is upon your head and pursuing your heels. Faithful God.

DAY 113

Your Will Be Done

Your kingdom come. Your will be done in earth, as it is in heaven.
Matthew 6:10

One day I was driving the car and everything seemed normal enough. Different cars were in their appropriate lanes as their drivers planned the route ahead. All of a sudden, out of nowhere, came the blaring of a fire engine siren and flashing lights. We all know what happens then. Drivers do their best to give way to the fire engine. There were a couple of cars that had to pull into a totally different lane than the one they were in. Other cars were pulled over to the side and parked in different directions, just to let the fire engine past. The scene afterwards was a lot different than before the fire engine arrived.

As I thought about this, I thought about the will of God. Sometimes life can be seemingly normal enough when, all of a sudden, God's will intervenes (just like the fire engine). And just as the cars had to get out of its pathway, so also, when God's will intervenes, then everything must get out of its pathway. Just as the plans of the drivers were changed and some even ended up in different directions, so it is also, when the will of God takes effect, that entire situations can be totally turned around and look completely different than before He intervened.

Today's verse says, 'Your will be done on earth as it is in Heaven.' God's will *shall* be done no matter what else happens. Maybe as a Christian, circumstances have come into your life and the situation looks hopeless. I want to remind you that God intervenes in the 'Red Seas' of our lives, and even they have to get out of the way when His will is done. Pharaoh's horses and chariots are stopped in their tracks when God steps into the situation.

Trying to stop the will of God is like trying to stop a river from flowing by holding up a teaspoon against it. The best place that you can be today is in the will of God. '*Your will be done in earth, as it is in heaven.*'

DAY 114

The Umpire's Chair

And let the peace of God rule in your hearts, to the which also you are called in one body; and be you thankful.
Colossians 3:15

Who loves watching tennis from Wimbledon? Granny McKinley had a friend whom she visited quite often, but this lady (in her 80s) told all of her friends that no-one was to call to see her during the two weeks that Wimbledon was in progress. She was an addict!

In 2019, there was a men's doubles match played that wasn't an official tournament game. It featured some older players. In the middle of the game, Frenchman Henri Le Conte needed a break so he called the umpire onto the court to take his place. Le Conte sat on the umpire's chair and gave commentary as the match continued. The umpire played alongside Le Conte's partner. It was all a bit of fun. But it's not really a good idea to allow one of the players of a doubles team to umpire a game because they will be slightly biased towards their own team!

In our verse we are told to let the peace of God rule in our hearts. The word for *'rule'* in Greek would have been very familiar to those living in Paul's day. It was used to depict an umpire at the Greek games. If there was a decision to be made in the contest, the umpire would decide. When Paul says to let the peace of God rule in your hearts, he means to let the peace of God be the umpire in your hearts. There are many battles that go on in our hearts every day. If we put *ourselves* on the umpire's seat in the battles of our hearts, we will usually make decisions that are biased towards our human thinking (which creates fear and anxiety by default).

Maybe we are fearful about a doctor's appointment, the well-being of a loved one, or starting a new job. When we put ourselves on the umpire's chair, we tend to choose worry. So, Paul is saying here to put God's peace on the umpire's chair and let God's peace make the final decision. Let God's peace rule in your heart.

DAY 115

Let It In

Let the word of Christ dwell in you richly in all wisdom; teaching and admonishing one another in psalms and hymns and spiritual songs, singing with grace in your hearts to the Lord.
Colossians 3:16

I will never forget the occasion: it was December and the snow was on the ground. Do you remember the days when it used to snow and lie on the ground for days or weeks? Nowadays it's gone almost the next day. They just don't make snow the way they used to! But the snow was on the ground, and you have got to imagine this small kitten that is black with white paws, and white bits on its nose and belly. It is beautiful and is crying at our back door. We were younger at the time and, because the house we lived in was really our grandmother's, we asked her permission to keep the kitten. She said, 'No, that kitten is not getting over the door of this house.' As time went on, we whined about it and she said, 'OK, only in the kitchen, but no farther.' Soon '*Kit*' was in the front room, up the stairs, and allowed access to the whole house, eventually becoming our pet for the next thirteen or so years. But before we could enjoy her presence, we had to let her in (or rather, Granny had to let her in!)

It's the same with the Word of God; you've got to let it in. Don't keep it outside the door of your life. Don't let it just have access to one compartment of your life, or a couple of compartments, but the whole '*house*'. Bring the wisdom of the Word of God into your personal life, your family life, and your work life. Paul says to let it dwell '*in*' you. This is not some sort of superficial reading of God's Word, but it is allowing the Word of God to go deep into your spirit and soul. We can do this in at least three ways. We can know and *memorise* it. Then, we can go deeper and seek to *understand* it. Lastly, once the Word is '*in*' us, we must let it *transform* us. Hebrews 4:12 reminds us that God's Word is cutting edge and goes deep into the secret places of our hearts. In what way has His Word transformed us in the last week?

DAY 116

Count Your Blessings

And whatsoever you do in word or deed, do all in the name of the Lord
Jesus, giving thanks to God and the Father by Him.
Colossians 3:17

In Colossians 3:15, Paul encourages us to be thankful. Then in verse 16, he encourages us to sing with gratefulness (or in other words, thankfulness). In verse 17, he tells us to give thanks to God. Three times in three verses, Paul has mentioned thankfulness so it must be very important.

Maybe you remember your mum or dad saying, 'If I've told you once; I've told you twice; don't let me have to tell you a third time!' You knew by then that what they were saying was very important! Here, Paul has to tell us for the third time. I wonder why? Does he know that we can be slow to be thankful? Someone has said to imagine if we only woke up with those things that we had thanked God for the day before, what would we have left? There is a hymn by Johnson Oatman that says, 'Count your blessings name them one by one,' but we are quicker to count our problems and name them one by one!

Over the summer, our girls went to a local summer scheme. One day I went to pick them up (I was slightly late) and immediately both of them fired three things at me that they weren't happy about. Ellie said that Karis was given a biscuit which she wasn't given. Karis won a game that she didn't win. And I was late picking them up! Karis' gripes were that she got accidentally hit on the nose. One of the helpers shouted at her. And I was late picking them up! They didn't count the fun they had, the good things they did, or the games they played. No, they just counted the problems.

When we think of how much God has done for us, surely we should be more thankful. Granny McKinley had her own variation on that old hymn I mentioned earlier. It went like this: 'Count your blessings, name them *four by four*. And you'll be surprised you had *so many more*!' Keep counting your blessings.

DAY 117

Whose Voice Are We Listening To?

My sheep hear My voice, and I know them, and they follow Me.
John 10:27

I was out for a couple of hours with the kids at some lakes and there was a big, long tree trunk in the grass. They were playing with it and trying to lift it. I warned them not to do so, as someone would get hurt. We walked a bit further. I turned my back for just a few moments and then I heard a loud, '*Wahhhhhhh!*' They had found another tree trunk, had been messing about with it, and Karis got hurt. If only they had listened to me, then there would have been no tears. How often has that scenario been played out? We tell them these things for their own good, but they choose to listen to that little voice in their head. Ellie used to say, 'My brain told me to do that!' We can laugh at this, but exactly the same scenario takes place in our own lives as adults.

Everything that is written in the Bible is given to us for our own good. We know that the voice of God is pure and perfect, but sometimes we listen to other voices. It goes way back to the Garden of Eden. Eve knew what God had said, but satan contradicted the Word of God and she had a decision to make as to which voice she would listen. She weighed it up and listened to the voice of satan over the voice of God. Jesus demonstrated the importance of listening to God's voice over the voice of satan when He faced temptation in the wilderness. Each time satan's voice tried to influence Jesus to do what he said, Jesus countered his voice with the Word of God. '*It is written.*'

Whose voice are we listening to? This is so important. Today, let's take stock of our thoughts. Have they been constantly negative? Have we slumped into discouragement and despair, or even sin? Counter false thoughts with the truth of the Word of God. Hear the voice of the Good Shepherd. Everything He tells us is for our own good so that we won't get hurt.

DAY 118

A Still, Small Voice

And after the earthquake a fire; but the LORD was not in the fire:
and after the fire a still small voice.
1 Kings 19:12

Elijah has just witnessed that one plus God is a majority. God has answered the prophets of Baal with fire upon the altar, and 450 of them are defeated. As we saw in a previous message (Day 33), Jezebel sends word that she is going to kill Elijah. The problem is that, even though Elijah has just seen God showing His power, he listens to the voice of Jezebel. The outcome of this is that he sits under a juniper tree and requests for himself that he might die. Aren't you glad God doesn't always answer our prayers when our minds are confused and frustrated?

Jezebel's words now dominate Elijah's thoughts and he has no one to counter those negative thoughts. You see, we read that he left his servant behind in Beersheba and then goes into the wilderness alone. Who knows, but if Elijah had brought his servant with him, he might have reminded him of the great victory that God had just brought about and encouraged him to keep on going. It's never a good thing for us to be alone for too long with our negative thoughts. Sometimes we just need someone to talk to. If you are tormenting yourself with thoughts of discouragement, can I urge you not to be alone with those thoughts? Find someone you can trust who has godly wisdom and talk these things out.

Most of all, we need to get to God's Word and get God's perspective on things. Later in the story, God came to Elijah in a still small voice and spoke to him. To hear a still small voice, you have to be quiet. If we want to hear the still, small voice of God, we need to get alone with Him, letting these negative voices in our head be quietened and hear what God wants to say. The Lord's perspective was that Elijah was not alone and seven thousand others had not bowed the knee to Baal. Let us get into the quietness and get God's perspective for our lives. Let's hear His voice.

DAY 119

The 'Walk With Jesus' Cap

*Now then we are ambassadors for Christ, as though God did beseech
you by us: we pray you in Christ's stead, be you reconciled to God.*
2nd Corinthians 5:20

I have a red baseball cap, given to me by a friend. The words,
'Walk With Jesus' are written on the front of it. A few years
ago, I went to Tyrella beach with Ellie, when she was smaller.
It was the Newcastle air show and you can usually get a good view
from the beach. All of a sudden, Ellie ran away from me. I called
for her to come back but she wouldn't. I ran after her and she
headed towards the sand dunes where people were sitting for a
good view of the airplanes. There was a piece of wire or something
in the grass. I tripped and fell embarrassingly headlong onto the
ground. I picked myself up and eventually caught Ellie. My pride
was wounded, having tripped in front of everyone. I was about to
give Ellie a good telling-off for not coming back after I had called
her (which had led to my fall!) Then I realised I had my *'Walk
With Jesus'* cap on. Imagine if I had given Ellie a piece of my
mind with that cap on. *'Walk With Jesus.'* That would not have
been a great advertisement!

In reality, as we live the Christian life, we should live it as if we
have a *'Walk With Jesus'* cap on all the time. Paul says that we are
ambassadors for Christ. An ambassador is expected to represent
his or her country in a good light and we are called to do the same
for Jesus. People judge our words, deeds, and attitudes (because
we take the Name of Jesus), whether we have a cap on us or not.

Let us by His grace and the power of His Spirit represent the Name
of Jesus well to a lost and dying world. Next time we have road
rage; next time we speak unkindly to someone; next time we are
about to gossip; remember that we are doing it, as it were, with our
'Walk With Jesus' cap on and the world is watching. The old
saying is true. The only Bible that many people will read is what
they will read through you and me.

DAY 120

All These Things Are Against Me!

All these things are against me.
Genesis 42:36

Granny McKinley was an amazing and very determined lady who had a lot of trials and difficulties in life. However, when she got to a very late stage of her life, she was still driving the car and really shouldn't have been. We had to speak to her on many occasions about giving it up. She had a saying which she used now and again. 'It's four against one in this house!' Of course, we weren't *against* her; this was for her own good and the good of other people who would be driving on the road. (She eventually stopped driving, by the way).

Jacob was thinking in this way also. He thought that all his circumstances were against him. Maybe we are thinking similarly. But this thinking can dangerously deteriorate to another level when we suppose that God is against us. Blow after blow can come in your life and you are literally on the floor. Then you may think, *'The other things I can just about take, but is God against me too?'* This is when many are tempted to walk away from God. We need to press in to God in times like this, rather than walk away.

Job lost everything: his family and his possessions. It seemed *everything* was against him. When he heard from his 'comforters', it seemed *everyone* was against him too. Then his wife almost brought him to a dangerous way of thinking when she told him to curse God and die. Surely God was against him? But he didn't do it, and later on we see the motivation behind Job's thinking, when he says that His Redeemer lives and one day, he will see Him face to face. Because his Redeemer lived, Job could face tomorrow.

Jacob's son, Joseph, gave the real perspective about what was going on in his father's life. He said to his brothers, 'You meant it for evil, but God meant it for good.' It may seem that people and circumstances are against you but know this today: God is *for* you. And since God is for you, who, then, or what, can be against you?

DAY 121

Moved With Compassion

But when He saw the multitudes, He was moved with compassion
on them, because they fainted, and were scattered abroad,
as sheep having no shepherd.
Matthew 9:36

I heard a recording of the late David Pawson, who told the following story. He had preached a moving sermon. A lady shook his hand at the door, saying, 'That moved me.' He replied, 'Oh? Where to?' The woman was incensed and left in a rage. That evening, he apologised for what he had said. The lady replied, 'No, you were right. After your words to me at the door, I went and *did something* about what I had heard you preach.' A sermon may move us, but it is only of any practical use if it moves us to *do something* and to put what we have learned into practice in our lives. The Lord, as He saw humanity in its sin, was not only moved with compassion, but He did something about it. He left Heaven's glory and died on a cross to set us free. In today's verse, Jesus saw a great multitude. He not only saw them but was moved with compassion towards them. He was not only moved with compassion but did something about it. He healed their sick.

If we want to be like Jesus, we need to be moved with compassion for a lost and dying world. How do we get this compassion? We won't learn it in a manual but will find it as we kneel before God and allow Him to soften our hearts. It is said that the Scottish preacher Robert Murray McCheyne constantly wept for his congregation in his study and in the pulpit. He was only following the example of his Saviour, Who wept over the city of Jerusalem.

Once we are moved with compassion for others, we should be moved to *do something*. CT Studd was a rich sportsman who was moved with compassion. He gave it all up to become a missionary in China, India, and Africa. He said, 'Some wish to live within the sound of church and chapel bell. I want to run a rescue shop within a yard of hell.' Have we been moved today? Where to?

DAY 122

What Is Your Mountain?

Therefore will not we fear, though the earth be removed,
and though the mountains be carried into the midst of the sea.
Psalm 46:2

The mountains of Mourne, which, as the timeless classic by Percy French says, 'Sweep down to the sea,' have been around for a long time! They have endured good days and bad days. We expect them to be there. Imagine if you turned on your TV one day and there was breaking news. There is a reporter standing with a camera crew in Newcastle, County Down, announcing that the mountains of Mourne have disappeared. They have indeed literally swept down into the sea. Imagine how that headline would play out in our world today. Psalm 46 describes a similar and almost apocalyptic scene. It talks about the mountains being carried into the sea. But the Psalmist says that even if such a nightmare situation should happen, he would not fear because God is his refuge and strength in trouble.

A mountain is always there. To our family, Dad was our mountain. He was always there. He was ill for around 40 years of his life (from his early thirties) but time after time, when there seemed to be an impossible situation medically, he always pulled through (of course, with God's help). It happened so many times, we almost got used to it. But in May 2011, something was different: Dad seemed battle-weary and the Lord called him home. That, for us, was like our mountain being removed. It was a catastrophic event for our family that would shake us up. Yet we found that even when the worst happened, God was our refuge and strength.

I don't know what *your* mountain is; something that was always there. Maybe it was a loved one, your health, or your job that has been removed and has shaken you to the very core. The Psalmist is encouraging you, even when the worst happens: don't fear. God will still be your refuge and strength, whatever comes your way.

DAY 123

The Trial Of Our Faith

Knowing this, that the trying of your faith works patience.
James 1:3

I recall being at a church praise service. A man was playing the organ as part of a praise group and within a few minutes, 'crash'; the stool collapsed. Down he went. To his credit, he got up quickly. Someone brought a chair and he continued as if nothing had happened. The service was being recorded for a *DVD* and I must confess that I asked for a copy. But the incident that I have related to you was edited out of it. Serves me right! It seemed that the stool was good enough to hold anyone. Perhaps it had been weakened over time, or a leg was loose. But it wasn't until that night that it became clear the stool wasn't able to stand up to the test. Sometimes our faith also has to be tested. It's not that God needs to see what our faith is like. He already knows. But *we need to see for ourselves* what it's like through testing and trials.

James says that the trying of our faith brings patience (or endurance). Paul also tells us in Romans 5:3-4, that trials produce patience, which in turn produces experience, which in turn produces hope. We are encouraged to take a long-term view of our trials. To take the short-term view will only leave us discouraged and downhearted. We are going through a process. When we exercise patience through a trial, we are really trusting that God knows best and that He will bring us through. Each time God brings us through a trial, this then builds up experience, which helps our faith the next time we go through a trial. This then gives us hope. Not a 'cross your fingers' hope; but when the Bible speaks of the Christian's hope, it is an *assured* hope.

Next time you are feeling like you are in a trial, remember it's not with the intended outcome that your faith should come crashing down like that stool. But it is designed to produce patience, experience, and hope. The end goal of it all is to bring maturity to our spiritual lives.

DAY 124

Centre Stage

*Then answered Peter, and said to Jesus, Lord, it is good
for us to be here: if You will, let us make here three tabernacles;
one for You, and one for Moses, and one for Elijah.*
Matthew 17:4

If Peter had been an actor, he surely would have been the leading man. He seemed to lead the disciples in what to say or do. Sometimes he either 'put his foot in it' by what he did, or 'put his mouth in it' by what he said. He was impulsive. Good old Peter, true to form, at the Transfiguration of Jesus, feels he has to say something. He blurts out, 'It is good for us to be here.' A bit of an understatement! Mark, in his account, explains that he didn't know what *to say*. Then, he suggests making three tabernacles. This time, Luke tells us that Peter didn't know what he *was saying*! We can sympathise with Peter. When holy moments come, we may not know what to say and may feel we have to *do* something. But it's OK to be quiet! Peter wants to freeze-frame this holy moment by making tabernacles. Had it been today, he might have wanted to get a film crew to make a video and then release it for others to enjoy. We read that while Peter was still speaking, God spoke. The Father interrupts and points them all to Jesus.

Although Peter meant well, he was really interfering in this holy moment. 'It is good for us to be here.' (*Whispering voice*: '*Yes, it is Peter, but it's not about us!*') Using the movie metaphor, Peter is like a supporting actor entering centre stage during the leading man's big moment. Although Peter is used to being the leading man around the disciples, when Jesus comes on the scene, he is only a supporting actor. Centre stage always belongs to Jesus. We need to get out of the way. The best thing Peter could have done would have been to quietly walk backward, out of centre stage, and bow in wonder and worship at this very holy of moments. The Transfiguration was a revealing of Jesus' glory. Our lives should be a revealing of His glory. But that can only happen when we get out of the way and let Jesus take centre stage in our lives.

DAY 125

Being With Him

Father, I will that they also, whom You have given Me, be with Me where I am; that they may behold My glory, which You have given Me: for You loved Me before the foundation of the world.
John 17:24

In 2019, we were in Portugal. I had to leave at the end of the week to go over to England for a conference. The rest of the family stayed on. I spent the first day in Birmingham before travelling to Malvern. It was Father's Day and I sat in a café, alone, on this special day (get the handkerchiefs out!) I really missed my family so much. I just wanted them to be with me. I'm sure you have felt the same way when separated from loved ones.

In John 17:24, Jesus is praying. His deep desire is that you and I be *with Him*. This is Jesus' High Priestly prayer before He goes to the cross. No doubt there is so much on His mind. But in that heartfelt prayer, the Lord thinks about you and me. He wants us so much to be in His Presence. Until that day comes, Jesus has given us the Holy Spirit to be with us, but that is not a permanent arrangement. The long-term goal is for us to be *with Him*. And guess what? Throughout the Bible, from Genesis to Revelation, His will is always done. It's going to happen! One day, we will be with Him! Nothing can stop it. Notice that Jesus doesn't say that we might be *where* He is, but that we might *be with Him*, where He is. You could get an invitation to Buckingham Palace, but not be where the King is. Jesus isn't just going to bring us to Heaven, but also, more importantly, to be with Him, personally. We look forward to being in that location, but Jesus will be what makes it Heaven for us.

Jesus then says that He wants us to behold His glory. If you get a new car or new furniture, one of the first things you want to do is to show it to those whom you love because you know that they will be genuinely happy for you. Jesus wants to show you His glory and for you to enjoy it with Him for all eternity. What an amazing time that will be.

DAY 126

Feasting While Being Cornered

You prepare a table before me in the presence of my enemies:
You anoint my head with oil; my cup runs over.
Psalm 23:5

You will have read previously about our cat. Unfortunately, she had a sad end. She was cornered by a snarling dog. In fear, she had a heart attack and died. In 2nd Samuel 17, David and those with him are escaping from the enemy, who were trying to corner them. They go into the wilderness and a group of people provide them with a feast in the middle of this desert place. Some think this incident is what David refers to in our verse today. (By the way, God can provide a feast for you in a spiritual wilderness. Sometimes he uses other people to do that. Maybe God has sent someone your way recently to help in a certain situation. Be aware also that God may call you to provide a physical or spiritual feast for someone else in their time of need).

Psalm 23:5 sees a sudden change in imagery from sheep to a banquet. Here, with the Psalmist surrounded by his enemies, the Lord prepares him a feast. What a picture. The enemy is outside the door and he is eating! Imagine if your house was surrounded by enemies and you shouted to your family, 'Will I put on the pan for a fry?' What would they think? Here is someone who is completely at ease, even though the enemy is snarling outside. Someone has said that the Lord fights for us while we eat. Then, the Lord anoints his head with oil. (Although shepherds anoint the sheep's head with oil to protect it from flies getting up its nose, the reference could also be to the custom of hospitality at that time. When a guest visited for a feast, you anointed their head with oil to refresh them and honour them). If you are feeling hemmed in by a snarling enemy, look out for a few things. Expect God to prepare a 'feast' for you. He may send someone to help you or do it Himself. Be prepared for Him to anoint you with the refreshing oil of the Holy Spirit, and to honour you, despite what the enemy is trying to do. In times of turmoil, have a heart of expectation. God loves you.

DAY 127

You Are What You Think

For as he thinks in his heart, so is he.
Proverbs 23:7

I'm sure you have heard the saying that '*You are what you eat.*' No doubt, you have heard someone say, 'I feel a lot healthier since I started eating salads.' That person was not me! If you are what you eat, then it could be argued that I'm morphing into a southern fried chicken! In our verse, Solomon is basically saying that you are *what you think about.* Jesus said that those things which proceed out of the mouth come from the heart. You *are* what is in your heart. If you are continually dwelling on negative things, you will most likely be a negative person. We all have a choice as to what we allow through our minds. Martin Luther is credited with saying that we can't stop the birds from flying above our heads, but we can stop them from making a nest in our hair! A wrong thought may come across our minds, but we have to decide whether to dwell on it or get rid of it and to nip it in the bud before it becomes something permanent. We don't really know the original source, but you have no doubt heard the saying that we should watch our thoughts because they become our words, which become our actions, which become our habits, which become our character, which becomes our destiny. It matters what we think.

We need to regulate our thoughts. Imagine a football game without any referee to regulate what happens on the pitch. There would be a free-for-all. It would be chaos. It's the same with our minds. There are some thoughts and we need to give them the 'red card', and send them straight off! Of course, we cannot do this on our own. We need the help of the Holy Spirit. Philippians 4:8 gives us a general rule of thumb as we sift through our thoughts. It tells us that whatever things are true, honest, right, pure, lovely, commendable, virtuous, or praiseworthy; think on these things. In Isaiah 26:3, we are assured that God will keep those in perfect peace whose minds are fixed on Him. There can be no higher form of thinking than this.

DAY 128

Don't Give The Enemy Your Keys

Submit yourselves therefore to God.
Resist the devil, and he will flee from you.
James 4:7

Granny McKinley had a gold *Austin Allegro* car. When she came to pick us up from school, some friends used to joke about the car because of its colour, and also because it was not considered to be a very good car. They nicknamed it '*Goldfinger*.' It was eventually given to me when I learned to drive. Despite its reputation and age, I liked it. One morning, however, when I went outside, I discovered that I had left my keys in the car the whole night. Of course, that prompted the jokes. 'You were hoping someone would take it away!' 'The car is so bad, that nobody will even take a free gift of it!'

When a nation is oppressed by an enemy, its people have two options. They can either submit or resist. With spiritual oppression, domineering thoughts can come from the evil one. It seems we are under constant attack and the enemy will try to wear us down until we submit. But the Word of God encourages us not to collaborate with these thoughts, but rather submit ourselves to God and resist the devil. When we submit to the enemy's oppressive lies, we open a door that allows him a foothold in our lives. *Going back to my opening illustration, it's like leaving a burglar the keys to our car and saying, 'Feel free to access what is mine.'*

Is the enemy telling you how worthless you are, or how hopeless your situation is? Have you been pulled into a dark spiral of negative thinking? Submit yourself afresh to God and what His Word says about you, rather than what the enemy says. Three times, Jesus quoted Scripture to the devil as He resisted His foe. What if you resist and he doesn't seem to leave? Our verse today says he *will* flee. Until he does, stand strong upon the Word of God. Don't give him the keys to your mind. You have a greater power within; the power of the Holy Spirit.

DAY 129

The Patience Of God

The Lord is not slack concerning His promise, as some men count slackness; but is longsuffering to us-ward, not willing that any should perish, but that all should come to repentance.
2nd Peter 3:9

You have a test at school and haven't prepared for it. As you go into school, you get a glimmer of hope as the teacher isn't there. But then you feel despair when the teacher walks in late. However, they don't mention the test for the first ten minutes and you think they have forgotten. All hopes are finally dashed as they hand out the papers for the test. Similarly, some people seem to think that because God hasn't judged the world yet, that He has forgotten, or isn't going to do it at all since it has been left for so long. Our verse tells us that God *hasn't* forgotten, but is holding His judgment back as He doesn't want anyone to perish.

I heard the story told of an atheist who openly challenged God that, if He was real, He should strike him down publicly, within sixty seconds. He took out his watch and, when the minute had elapsed, he triumphantly proclaimed to the crowd that there was no God. A lady who had watched that scene was concerned as to why nothing happened and asked her minister about it. He replied, 'Ah, do you think that man could have exhausted the love of God in just sixty seconds?' Two thousand years have almost passed since Jesus was nailed to the cross, and still God holds out His offer of mercy.

God is not willing that *any* should perish. You could easily read over the word *'any'* without realising that in the original Greek it has the idea of a person as an individual, and not just a random person. God cares for the individual. He cares for you. Such was the passion of His heart in not wanting you to perish forever, that He sent His Son to die on a cross for you. Romans 2:4 reminds us that the goodness of God leads us to repentance. When we take that good road of repentance, the way of the cross leads us home. There's hope for *'the any.'* There's hope for you.

DAY 130

No Condemnation

There is therefore now no condemnation to them which are in Christ Jesus, who walk not after the flesh, but after the Spirit.
Romans 8:1

Romans 8 is an amazing chapter. It begins with '*no condemnation*' and it ends with '*no separation.*' It is true, in the case of most Christians that, at some point along the line, either our own conscience, another person, or the accuser satan himself, will come and accuse us of our past. Isn't it amazing that we are quicker to remember our past sins than God is? God says that He will remember our sins and iniquities no more; but it seems that we remember them forever! I wonder, as Paul wrote these words in Romans 8, did he ever have flashbacks to when he persecuted the church? We don't know. But what we do know is that Paul had a wonderful grasp in his spirit about what exactly had taken place when he came to Jesus for salvation. He knew that he had been set free from condemnation.

However, there are a lot of Christians who, while they are totally assured that their unsaved past is gone, are troubled by things they have done wrong *since* they got saved. They understand that before they were saved, they didn't really know any better, but now since they have been saved, they feel guilty because at times they do things that are wrong. None of us are perfect. The first epistle of John was initially written to believers and not the unsaved. This is for us. John says that if we confess our sins, He is faithful and just to forgive us our sins and to cleanse us from all unrighteousness. Get some words into your mind. '*Faithful*' - He will forgive every time. '*Just*' – He can do it legally. No one can come back and accuse you. '*All*' – He will forgive every single sin. '*Cleanse*' – when you have confessed and received forgiveness, instead of feeling condemned, you should feel cleansed. Maybe some believer reading these words has been tormented by condemnation. Exchange that condemnation for cleansing right now. *No condemnation* for those who are in Christ Jesus.

DAY 131

More Than Conquerors

Nay, in all these things we are more than conquerors through Him that loved us.
Romans 8:37

I'm going to teach you a Greek word. Are you excited? You will recognise it: '*Nike*'. There was a Greek (so-called) goddess called *Nike*, which represented victory. Some of you may have sportswear which bears that name. Now you know what it means. *Victory*! A form of that Greek word is used in today's verse to bring us the word '*conqueror*', which describes the Christian. Now, that's good. But do you know what is even better? We are described as '*more than conquerors!*' In my mind, there's something supernatural going on here. You are either a conqueror or not a conqueror. But when we come into the territory of '*more than conqueror*,' it's only Jesus Who can do that.

Maybe you are reading this and you are thinking, '*I don't feel like a conqueror, never mind more than a conqueror.*' Well, look at the children of Israel as they came to the banks of the Jordan river. God had said forty years previously that every place the sole of their foot would tread, He would give to them. They were conquerors and they hadn't even set foot on the other side. I'm sure they didn't feel like conquerors, just as you don't. Joshua and Caleb had been waiting forty years since that original promise was made and now, they face obstacles, including giants. Surely, they feel like giving up. But Joshua and Caleb are still living the life of conquerors. That victory is just as real to them now as it was forty years before when they were first promised it. They haven't even physically won it yet, but they trust God and live in faith, as if they have already received it. And receive it, they do.

Yes, you are more than a conqueror. But there's one part to this that is *so* vital. We are only conquerors 'Through Him that loved us.' Take away Jesus; take away the cross and we are nothing. There's (*more than*) victory in Jesus!

DAY 132

The Whole Point Of The Story

When Jesus saw their faith, He said to the sick of the palsy,
Son, your sins be forgiven you.
Mark 2:5

This hasn't happened to me (yet!), but it must be very frustrating for someone who is preaching (maybe on the love of God) to be told by someone that they enjoyed what was said about fasting! You have been preaching your heart out for thirty minutes and someone has picked up one word that you only mentioned in passing. They have missed the whole point of your message.

It can be very easy to miss the point of today's passage. Is it about this man's friends bringing him to Jesus? That's part of it but not the main point. What about his healing? Some Bibles entitle this passage '*The healing of the paralytic.*' Great heading but not the main point. The main point is that a man's sins were forgiven by Jesus. He probably thought that the greatest words he could ever hear would be, 'Be healed.' But even if he had only been healed, one day he would die and go to meet God. He had a greater need which Jesus addressed. Listen to the tenderness of Jesus. 'Son, your sins be forgiven you.' Jesus knew exactly what he needed.

In a previous job, I was the annoying person who cold-called people and tried to sell them mobile phones. I have extolled the virtues of the latest smartphone, waxed eloquent concerning its multi-megapixel camera, super-fast processor, and slick touch screen, only to be told by an 80-year-old grandmother that she has no need for it, as she only makes emergency phone calls! I could only sell to those who saw their need for a better phone. We *think* we know what we need: a bigger house, a better job, or more money. But Jesus knows that we have a greater need: forgiveness. He longs to give it to us today. But we can only receive it when we *see our need.* When we do, then we will see the point of the story of why Jesus had to die. It was so that we could be *forgiven.*

DAY 133

A Surprise Visit

*Now Moses kept the flock of Jethro his father-in-law, the priest of
Midian: and he led the flock to the backside of the desert,
and came to the mountain of God, even to Horeb.*
Exodus 3:1

Some time ago on the news, we saw some scenes from the
mountains of Mourne where there were some fires which
had broken out. It looked quite frightening. When I saw it,
my mind turned to the burning bush where God appeared to
Moses. This meeting with God was, of course, something that
Moses would never forget and would change his life forever. We
all desire those sorts of life-changing experiences with God, but I
want you to notice the circumstances in Moses' life at the time this
meeting took place. Moses got a glimpse of God's glory, not in a
palace in Egypt, but in the backside of the wilderness, tending
sheep. We are usually waiting for the Presence of God to show up
in a special way when we are in some great church service, or
when our hearts are filled with praise and worship, or when our life
seems to be going well. But God has a tendency to make surprise
visits when we least expect it.

Isaiah was given a glimpse of the Lord in all of His glory at a time
of national mourning following the death of King Uzziah. He also
showed up to Elijah when he was in the throes of depression. The
Lord came to him, not in the earthquake, nor the fire, but in a still,
small voice. He made Himself visible to the three Hebrew men in
the fiery furnace when their situation looked hopeless.

Maybe you feel your life at the moment is uneventful as you slog
away, working hard from day to day. Don't be discouraged. It is in
moments like these that God tends to show up and give us
glimpses of Himself. Why? Because it is in moments like these
that we are humble and our hearts are ready to hear from God.
Don't knock the wilderness experience. You will most likely learn
more about God in the wilderness than in the palace.

DAY 134

If Only

And when he came to himself, he said, How many hired servants of my father's have bread enough and to spare, and I perish with hunger!
Luke 15:17

Travel agencies often warn against travelling to certain hotspot destinations, especially during a war or political unrest. If there was such a thing as a spiritual travel agency, I have no doubt that it would warn us against the following dangerous hotspot destination. It's a place that will cause you emotional agony. It will hinder your spiritual growth for sure. It has even been known to lead to premature death, through suicide. This dangerous hot spot destination is called, '*If Only*', and is in proximity to another hotspot destination called '*Guilt*'. '*If only I hadn't made that wrong choice in life.*' '*If only I hadn't spoken those harsh words.*' '*If only I had been there when my loved one died.*'

In Luke 15, the prodigal son came to this destination hotspot, '*If Only*'. As he found himself in the darkest of places, he didn't use the exact words, but, in effect, he was saying, '*If only I hadn't left my father's house. If only I hadn't treated my father in such a terrible way.*' The prodigal, in the destination hotspot of '*If Only*', had one of two choices. The first choice was to stay there and be caught in a never-ending cycle of guilt and despair. He took the second option. We read that he arose and went to a different destination: his father's house. Home.

If you find yourself imprisoned in the destination of '*If Only*', the solution is to arise and go to your Heavenly Father. Give that '*If Only*' to Him and be released from the guilt that it brings.

Sometimes when there is trouble in a destination, embassies call on their citizens to leave that country immediately. I have no doubt that God is calling His people out of the destination of '*If Only*'. Get out now. It's urgent. Escape to your Heavenly Father, and leave your '*If Only*' in His Hands.

DAY 135

What If?

*If My people, which are called by My name, shall humble themselves,
and pray, and seek My face, and turn from their wicked ways; then will I
hear from heaven, and will forgive their sin, and will heal their land.*
2nd Chronicles 7:14

In the previous message we looked at how the two words, '*If
Only*', can lead us into a dark place. In effect, they really close
doors in our lives and our spiritual experiences because they
cause us to withdraw into ourselves, causing negative thinking.
However, today I want to look at two words that will *open* doors
and enhance our spiritual walk with the Lord. They are the words,
'*What If?*'

2nd Chronicles 7:14 is probably the best-known '*What If?*' in the
Bible. *What if* God's people humble themselves, repent, and pray?
God encourages us with the amazing possibilities which can
happen if we go through with this. He will hear, forgive, and heal.

But I want to just look generally at this concept, '*What if God's
people?*' What if God's people made a conscious decision to love
those who hate us and to forgive those who have sinned against
us? What if God's people made a phone call to someone who is
lonely? What if we intentionally walked alongside someone going
through a dark valley? What if we sent a brother or sister in the
Lord an encouraging text today? What if God's people took the
gospel to the needy, prayed for those who are sick, read their
Bibles consistently and sought God intimately in prayer?

Each one of us has some aspect in our lives where we are lacking.
In front of us stands a door. That door is called, 'What If?' Now,
here is the important bit. The blessing doesn't come in its fullness
to those who just stand outside the door and look at it, but to those
who open it and go through it. God is challenging each of us in our
own lives with a 'What If?' Can I encourage you to walk through
that door and watch what God does in that situation? '*What If?*'

DAY 136

Why?

And about the ninth hour Jesus cried with a loud voice, saying,
Eli, Eli, lama sabachthani? that is to say,
My God, My God, why have You forsaken Me?
Matthew 27:46

The last couple of messages have been looking at two sets of words. Today it is one word. It is small to look at on a page, but gigantic when it enters our hearts and is usually called out in the middle of a crisis. It is the question, *why?* Although this is a question that most times we cannot answer, we, as God's people do have a source of help in the midst of this question.

Firstly, the Bible tells us Jesus was acquainted with grief. He walked hand in hand with grief. He knows what we are going through when this question rises in our hearts. *Secondly*, we read also that Jesus wept (John 11:35). The Bible encourages us to weep with those who weep. Jesus knows what it is like to enter into grief with others. *Thirdly*, in Matthew 27:46, we read that Jesus asked this question Himself when He cried out to His Father, 'Why have You forsaken Me?' And just as we don't seem many times to have any answers to our question *why*, did you ever notice that Jesus doesn't get an answer? We can make a theological attempt at an answer, but God and the Scriptures are silent on this question.

I mentioned (on Day 23) that Horatio Spafford lost four daughters in a tragic sea disaster. He wrote a hymn that didn't even ask the reason *why*, or attempt to answer the question, but simply stated that 'When sorrows like sea billows roll,' then 'it is well with my soul.' We may not receive answers to our question, *why*, down here, but we have God's peace to comfort us until we reach Heaven. Some say it will be then that they will get an answer to the question *why*. But my dad (who suffered severe illness himself for 40 years) always contended that we won't need answers because we will be standing face to face with Jesus. Then, all our questions will surely have faded away, as we stand in His perfect Presence.

DAY 137

Waking Up

As for me, I will behold Your face in righteousness:
I shall be satisfied, when I awake, with Your likeness.
Psalm 17:15

The following is a true story. There was an Australian woman who went for a tonsil operation in 2021 and, when she woke up from surgery, she was speaking with an Irish accent! Apparently, it is meant to be a real, but rare condition, called *Foreign Accent Syndrome*, which could be related to the brain or the immune system.

As I thought about the change that this lady experienced when she woke up from surgery, my mind went to an even greater transformation that awaits the Christian, when they pass from this world to the next. David says in Psalm 17:15, 'I shall be satisfied, when I awake, with Your likeness.' What a transformation. To go to sleep and to wake up with the likeness of the Lord.

But you will wake up to some other amazing things. You will awaken in a place of '*no mores*'. No more tears; no more death; no more sorrow; no more pain. But even more amazing is the fact that when we open our eyes for the first time in Heaven, we (as John puts it) shall see Jesus as He is. What an awakening!

My mind turned to Fanny Crosby, the blind hymn writer who gave us hymns such as 'Blessed Assurance.' She lived her 94 years in a world of darkness. She never saw the sky, the trees, or the sea. She never saw a human face. But when she first opened those eyes in Heaven, what a moment, as she gazed on the face of her Saviour.

Acts 7:60 tells us that as Stephen was being stoned to death, he prayed for those who were stoning him and then we read, 'He fell asleep.' What beautiful comfort it is to think that our loved ones who have died in Christ simply fell asleep and woke up in the Presence of Jesus. No wonder Paul cried out, 'O grave, where is your victory?' Death simply ushers the Christian straight into Heaven. Absent from the body, present with the Lord.

DAY 138

A Weight Off Your Shoulders

Then he answered and spoke to me, saying,
This is the word of the LORD to Zerubbabel, saying,
Not by might, nor by power, but by My Spirit, says the LORD of hosts.
Zechariah 4:6

Zerubbabel was a man with a name that was very hard to pronounce! He also must have had a lot of stress in his life and a heavy weight upon his shoulders. It was Zerubbabel's task to rebuild the temple. It must have seemed that everything was all down to him. How would he ever get this job done? But God is so gracious and sends an angel to him. The angel assures him that it's not by might, nor by power, but by the Spirit of the Lord that it will be done. I can almost hear the weight falling off his shoulders! Yes, he is still going to oversee the project; he is still going to do the best he can; he still has great responsibility. But what a feeling of liberation Zerubbabel must have had when he realised that the results were ultimately not down to him, but that God was going to send His help and power to get the work done.

Sometimes we try to do things in our own power. Abraham was promised an Isaac, but he tried to take things into his own hands and he produced an Ishmael, the result being that trouble and strife came into the family. The whole thing wasn't really resolved until Ishmael was sent away. What happens when we try to do things in our own strength and by our own cleverness, is that we produce our Ishmaels which get in the way of what God is trying to do in our lives. We have to repent of those things and clear the pathway for God to do what He wants to do.

When serving God, you don't have to do things by your own power. Don't panic. Just be faithful and keep on doing what God has called you to do. Try not to get too stressed about it. While you have a part to play, ultimately the results are not down to you but to God. Let that weight fall off your shoulders when you realise that the job will get done by His might and His power.

DAY 139

Let Go

Be still, and know that I am God:
I will be exalted among the heathen, I will be exalted in the earth.
Psalm 46:10

When Ellie was just a baby, it was so difficult to get her to sleep. I would pace up and down for at least an hour, singing all the nursery rhymes and kids' choruses I could think of. Then, when it would seem as if she was eventually sleeping, I would bring her to the cot. In a manoeuvre akin to something from *Mission Impossible*, I would lower her slowly down towards the cot. Once her body reached the cot itself, I gently removed my hands from under her tiny body, and turned to softly walk out the door without making the floorboards squeak. It was generally at this moment of exit that Ellie would wake up, almost instinctively, and cry the house down. I was back to square one. If only she would stop struggling, and sleep!

When the Psalmist says, '*Be still,*' it actually doesn't mean to stand still or even to be quiet (although both can be involved). This command means to stop striving, or to '*let it go*'. The context of this verse is the heathen nations fighting against God. The call to be still could be one of two things. It could be a call for the nations to stop striving against God because He will be exalted before them. But it could also be spoken to God's people. You see, it is possible that the people of Israel were getting anxious and worked up about the heathen nations, and God is calling on them to '*let it go*', stop struggling; know that He is God, and trust in Him.

So often in the struggles of our lives, we find it hard to let things go and to commit them fully to God. We sometimes try to work things out ourselves and get nowhere. We toss things over and over in our minds, which makes us even more anxious. God is calling us to stop struggling, to stop striving, and give the situation to Him. That might involve us being quiet. It may involve us being still. But whatever it takes, let it go and let God take over.

DAY 140

A Provoking Parable

Should not you also have had compassion on your fellow servant,
even as I had pity on you?
Matthew 18:33

Jesus tells us a parable about a king who took account of his servants. One of them owed him (in today's money) millions of pounds. The servant and his family were going to be sold so that payment could be made. He pleaded with the king for time to pay it back. The king was moved with compassion and forgave the debt. That same servant, who was forgiven this great debt, refused to forgive one of his fellow servants who owed him around £200, and threw him into prison. When the king heard this, he was angry and put the unforgiving servant in prison until his debt was paid.

It is so easy to be like this servant and forget how much we have been forgiven by God. We can throw people into the prison of our minds by not forgiving them for their sins against us. This parable is meant to provoke us to see ourselves in the story. It's like someone who is prodding us with a poker. You may remember the parable that Nathan told David about the rich man who had many cattle and sheep, and needed to make a meal for someone. He took a poor man's lamb, the only lamb he had, and used it for the meal. David was angry and said the man should die. Nathan dramatically turned to him and said, in effect, *'You are the man, David. This parable is all about you.'* The parable had been told to provoke David and prod at him, until he saw his guilt (see 2nd Samuel 12).

We have been forgiven the greatest debt by God for our sins; yet sometimes we refuse to forgive others a lesser sin in comparison to what God has forgiven us. Although we put that person in a prison of our minds, *we* are the ones who are really imprisoned. This parable is perhaps provoking and prodding at us today. It is meant to. When we look at Calvary, how can we not forgive others? God can give us the grace to forgive. We will feel a heavy burden lifted off our shoulders and can walk in liberty once again.

DAY 141

Not Ashamed

For I am not ashamed of the gospel of Christ:
Romans 1:16

Di and I went to Tullymore Forest in Newcastle with her late uncle José, (who was a great man with a heart of gold). Some kids were fishing at a lake and didn't seem to be having any success, so José asked if he could help to show them how it is done. They gave him a fishing rod; he threw it way back, and the line went up into the tree above them and got tangled around it. We felt like slipping quietly away and pretending we didn't know him! We've often laughed about that one ever since.

I wonder are there times when the gospel has come up in a conversation and we've been embarrassed, and felt like quietly slipping away? No doubt it has happened to us all. But when you think about it, the gospel is good news. Why should we be ashamed of the greatest news that any ear could ever hear; that sets people free? We should proclaim it from the rooftops.

Proverbs 11:26 says that if someone withholds corn from the people, they will end up cursing him. Imagine that you are starving. You come to my house and I'm eating a fast-food bargain bucket (10 pieces) all by myself. There's plenty for both of us and you are drooling at the mouth, but I don't give you a crumb! What would you think of me?

We have the gospel in our hearts. There is more than enough for the whole world and yet we sometimes withhold that spiritual food from others because we are worried about what people think of us. In regards to the pulpit, if a preacher never preaches the gospel, it is like a doctor who never writes a prescription, or a surgeon who never performs a surgery. What's the point? Paul says there is a woe upon himself if he doesn't preach the gospel (1st Corinthians 9:16). Never be ashamed of the good news. It is the power of God to break men's and women's chains. Jesus wasn't ashamed of us when He hung on the cross; let us not be ashamed of Him.

DAY 142

The Gospel Truth

For I am not ashamed of the gospel of Christ:
for it is the power of God to salvation to every one that believes;
to the Jew first, and also to the Greek.
Romans 1:16

The epistle to the Romans was written when the greatest power on the face of the earth was Rome. Christians were living right in the middle of this powerful empire. Paul is reminding them that there is a greater power even than Rome: the power of the gospel. The Greek word here for '*power*' is where we get the word for '*dynamic*'. The true gospel has the dynamic to transform lives.

The motivational gospel tells you that *'You can do it; you can do it. You have the power within yourself to do whatever you want to do.'* However, Jesus said that without Him, we can do nothing. Jesus alone has the power to change lives.

The prosperity gospel is focused on a different power - the power of wealth and money. Enough said!

The social gospel is kind; and yes, of course, it is right to help people who are worse off than ourselves. But that should be the outworking of the true gospel anyway. Once you are truly saved, you will want to help others. However, a 'works' gospel in itself has no power to change lives.

The moral gospel is where we try to live as good a religious life as we can; but, no matter how well we try to live, this cannot remove our past sins and those we will commit in the future. We need a Saviour.

The true gospel is marked by the power to save and transform lives; to take the dead in sin and miraculously make them alive to God. That is the litmus test which determines whether a gospel is true or false. Motivation, prosperity, social awareness and morality cannot do this. Only the true gospel of Jesus Christ can. We need a Saviour.

DAY 143

The Gates Of Hell Shall Not Prevail

And I say also to you, That You are Peter, and upon this rock I will build
My church; and the gates of hell shall not prevail against it.
Matthew 16:18

No doubt you have seen a parent play with a child by putting their hand on top of the child's head and asking them to try and hit back. Of course, they will try as hard as they can and use up all their energy, but they will not be successful as they are being held at arm's length by the parent's long arm. The child will not be able to prevail. Jesus said that He would build His church and the gates of hell shall not prevail against it. You see, satan can use all his energy in trying to destroy the church, but he is being held at an arm's length by the Lord and he cannot destroy Jesus' church.

The church in China, as we know, has been sent underground. You would think, logically, that this would cause the church to dwindle. But it is generally accepted that the Chinese church is on course to become one of the world's largest churches within the next twenty years or so. Its numbers may even exceed those of the church in America at a future time. Dark days or persecution do not determine the growth of the church. The Lord dictates the growth of the church because Jesus called it '*My church.*' What the Master-builder has constructed, no one will be able to take down. The greatest force in the world today is not a military, political, or even religious one. But the greatest force today on planet earth is the church of the Living God, marching to the drumbeat of their commander and chief, Jesus Christ; directed by the leading and the power of the Holy Spirit.

Let's work then, knowing that the enemy cannot overcome the church of Jesus Christ. You see, when you read the very last book of the Bible, you will read that Jesus wins! He has the final say. Thrones will perish and kingdoms will fall, but the church of Jesus Christ shall prevail.

DAY 144

Do You Know It?

But that you may know that the Son of man
has power on earth to forgive sins,
Mark 2:10

There are some people who, when you tell them you have received forgiveness of sins, say that you are being very presumptuous. They claim that no one can know for sure they are forgiven until the next life. Granny McKinley, as a young lady many years ago, got saved. She told her minister. Instead of him being happy for her, he as much as insinuated that she had lost her mind and she didn't need to be saved in the first place. Needless to say, she never went back!

Some people say that you have to do the best you can and, in a future day, God will weigh up your good deeds against your bad deeds, and only then will you know if you are saved. However, to bring our good works to God is an insult to Him. It is to misunderstand the seriousness of sin, and to say that Jesus didn't need to die on the cross. You can know that you are forgiven here and now. You don't have to wait and hope for the best. John said in 1 John 5:13 that he was writing to the believers that they may *know* they have eternal life. It can be a blessed certainty. You can sing Fanny Crosby's words, '*Blessed assurance, Jesus is mine.*'

In our verse today, Jesus wants people to *know* that He has the power on earth to forgive sins. This word, '*know*', in the original Greek, denotes not merely head knowledge, but knowing beyond the shadow of a doubt. Maybe as you read this, satan is making you doubt your forgiveness. Someone has said that, whenever the devil opens his mouth to speak, fill it with the Word of God and leave him to choke on it! Listen rather to Jesus, Who says He has the power to forgive sins, and He wants you to *know* it beyond the shadow of a doubt. If you have come to Jesus in repentance and through faith in His work on the cross, then you are forgiven. Believe it and *know* it.

DAY 145

Acknowledge Him

Trust in the LORD with all your heart;
and lean not to your own understanding.
In all your ways acknowledge Him, and He shall direct your paths.
Proverbs 3:5,6

Hebrew is a very pictorial language. The root word for *'trust'* has the picture of a family at home and at rest, surrounded by strong walls. It is a picture of security and peace. When we trust God, we are resting 'inside the four walls' of His peace and security. But we have to do it with all our heart (which is the command centre of our being). In war, the enemy will do all they can to attack the command centre and to create havoc. That's why it is so important to give God control of our command centre and to rest in His security. We also have to avoid the mistake of leaning on our own understanding. It is said that many want to serve God, but only in an advisory capacity! Imagine us, mere humans, trying to give counsel to the all-wise God! If we lean on His understanding, it will hold us securely.

Then, we have to acknowledge Him in all our ways. We used to have fun explaining to visitors from abroad that if they are walking down a street in Northern Ireland and a stranger makes a motion with their head to the one side, they haven't taken a cramp in their neck but they are simply acknowledging them. They might add the words, 'What about ye?' Acknowledging God in this verse is not indicating a polite nod of the head to the Almighty but it means to know Him intimately and to give Him full access to our lives.

If we do these things, God will direct our paths. The phrase *'direct your paths'* can be translated also as *'make your paths smooth.'* It doesn't mean you will live a trouble-free life, but that God will smooth out obstacles in your path and make a way for you. He did it with Joseph, who found himself in a pit and then a prison. But God smoothed the path and led him to a palace. God is making a path for you that will one day lead to the palace of the King.

DAY 146

There, There, There

Have not I commanded you? Be strong and of a good courage;
be not afraid, neither be you dismayed:
for the LORD your God is with you wherever you go.
Joshua 1:9

When kids are scared, parents might put a loving arm around them and bring comfort, saying, '*There, there, there, everything is going to be OK.*' However, it works differently with adults. We can meet some people going through terrible situations in life, and our '*There, there, there,*' just doesn't work because we aren't really sure how things are going to turn out. But to the child of God, we can give them the words of this verse with assurance and tell them not to be afraid or dismayed because the Lord is with us wherever we go. He's in that doctor's waiting room; He's in that difficult work situation; He's in that darkened room, as you cry yourself to sleep. *Wherever you go.*

A mistake we can sometimes make is to think that God is just with us when things are going well. But God was just as much with Joseph when he was sold into slavery as when he was a free man. Even in faraway Egypt, we see that Joseph found favour with Potiphar. God was working things for Joseph's good in a very bad situation. He is with you in the difficult times too.

A golden retriever lived across the road from us. I loved him to bits. Goldie was a big coward when it came to cats! He would be sitting at the front gate and the local cat would come strutting past in all her majesty. Goldie would put his head down, cower away in fear and slither up the driveway, hoping that she hadn't noticed him. However, when the kids with whom he lived came out to play, he was a completely different dog. He would have chased the cat up the road, no problem at all. What made the difference? It was the presence of those whom he loved and felt safe with. If we can get a grasp of this today, that the eternal God is *with us*, it's going to change how we react to different situations in our lives.

DAY 147

A Strange Place For Prayer

Then Jonah prayed to the LORD his God out of the fish's belly.
Jonah 2:1

Have you ever had a near-death experience? I had one similar to Jonah, minus the fish! I was in Switzerland on Lake Thun (in Interlaken), which is in the top ten of the largest lakes in Switzerland. We were on a dinghy, which was tied to the back of a boat. My Swiss cousins and I were sitting on the edge of the dinghy and the edge was wet. One minute we were talking, and the next minute I was away! Like Jonah, I went down, down, down. I couldn't swim and had no life jacket on. I thought this was '*it*'. I thought I was going to die. Somehow, I pushed myself upwards, emerging almost right beside the dinghy and they grabbed me. It all happened so quickly. When we got to the land, we all formed a circle and prayed and thanked God for His mercy.

One of the strangest beginnings to a chapter of the Bible is Jonah Chapter 2. Jonah is having a near-death experience. '*Then Jonah prayed to the LORD his God out of the fish's belly.*' People have prayed in massive churches or in places with beautiful surroundings, but very few from the belly of a fish! Jonah is at rock bottom. Ever since he decided to run from the Lord, his life has been on a downward spiral. He went *down* to Joppa, *down* into the boat, and then the sailors threw him *down* into the sea. His physical journey *downwards* is a picture of his spiritual state. This is what happens when we run from God.

What's the worst place you have prayed from (spiritually, not physically)? Have you ever hit rock bottom? Has life ever taken twists and turns and brought you into a horrible place? But you prayed. Yes, *you prayed*. And here is a simple truth today. No matter how bad your situation seems to be, *pray*. In your darkest moment. In a time of grief. When you are feeling lonely. When you get bad news. Whatever the situation. God hears prayers, even from the belly of a fish!

DAY 148

The Greatest Upgrade Of All

Behold, I shew you a mystery;
We shall not all sleep, but we shall all be changed.
1st Corinthians 15:51

Di and I went to Paris for our honeymoon in September 2007, and the rugby World Cup was underway. Imagine our horror when the hotel receptionist informed us that he had no record of our booking. The hotel eventually said they could give us a room for one night only, but we would have to find somewhere else afterwards. Paris was full of rugby fans and we could imagine spending the next day going around the city looking for somewhere to stay, only to be told they were booked up due to the rugby. Our hearts sank. The tiny room they gave us also had a stale, smoky smell. The next morning, I was straight on to the company in England whom I had paid for the holiday. To make a long story short, they admitted they had received my money and the person who was dealing with it had forgotten to book the hotel and pay them the money. We were informed that we would stay in one of the best rooms in the hotel for the rest of our holiday! The room was beautiful and we thanked God for the amazing *upgrade*.

One day, God is going to give His people an even more amazing upgrade and it will happen in a moment, in the twinkling of an eye. Paul says that we *shall* all be changed. He said, 'This corruptible *must* put on incorruption, and this mortality *must* put on immortality.' Note the words of certainty in italics. There is nothing that can stop this. Why? Paul goes on to say that death has been swallowed up in victory. You see, because Jesus rose again, we shall rise again also. Jesus is coming again, and He will give us an '*upgrade*'. We will be given a glorious body like His. We will go to a place of many mansions which He has prepared for us. We shall never sin, never die, never cry. Down here on earth we trust a Saviour Whom we cannot physically see; but then we will *see Him* face to face. That will be the greatest upgrade of them all!

DAY 149

Magnifying God Or Our Problems?

O magnify the LORD with me, and let us exalt His name together.
Psalm 34:3

I will never forget the day I looked down the barrel of a gun in my place of employment. Although there was a partition between myself and the person with the gun, it was still frightening. Afterwards, I was asked to give a statement to the police and, if I recall correctly, I said the person with the gun was about 6 ft 1. It turned out he was just medium height, maybe around 5 ft 6 or 5 ft 7. But with that gun in his hand, he sure looked a lot bigger to me! Sometimes, while our problems may be big, we can tend to magnify them to a greater degree than what they really are. Fear, worry, and panic usually cause us to do so. However, when we magnify God in our lives, it seems that our problems are put into perspective.

When the children of Israel came to spy out the land, ten of the spies saw big problems. There were giants in the land, the people were strong, and there were walled cities. The spies said they felt like grasshoppers in comparison to these giants. Caleb thought differently. He said that they should go and possess the land. Two different perspectives. God said that Caleb had a different spirit in him than the others. Yes, the problem might have been big but, in perspective, Caleb's God was much bigger.

David says to magnify the Lord and exalt His Name. To magnify the Lord means to make Him big in our lives. If you are out for a drive in the car and you see some mountains, the farther away you are from them, the smaller they seem to be. However, the closer you get to them, then the bigger they seem to be. The closer we get to God, then the greater He will be in our hearts and minds. Although we may have big problems, we will realise that God is bigger than our biggest problem. When David magnified the Lord, in the following verse we read that He delivered him from all his fears. He can do it for us too.

DAY 150

Rolling The Credits

All my state shall Tychicus declare to you, who is a beloved brother,
and a faithful minister and fellow servant in the Lord:
Colossians 4:7

At the end of a movie, the credits roll up the screen, listing those who helped make the movie possible. Ironically, very few people look at the credits. At the *Oscar* ceremony, famous actors and actresses receive their awards and make an acceptance speech. They thank assistants, script writers, those from the costume department and many more. After getting tearful when mentioning their mum or dad, they usually say, "Without these people none of this would be possible."

At the end of Paul's letter to the Colossians, the credits are rolling. There is a list of ten names of people who helped to make Paul's ministry possible. We would tend to just read over them quickly and not think anything of them. Paul got a lot of the credit for what was carried out in his ministry, but he had a network of people without whom things would have been much more difficult. These men were people of character. Tychicus was someone who was dependable. Aristarchus went through thick and thin with Paul. He was almost killed in a riot and was there with Paul in a shipwreck. He ended up being a fellow-prisoner. He was sold out for God. Epaphras was a man who was passionate in prayer. Mark was someone who bounced back from failure and had a fruitful ministry. These, and more, were the backbone of Paul's ministry.

It is similar in the church. The minister's name may be on the noticeboard, but it is the unnamed members of the congregation who are the backbone of all that goes on in the church (by the power of the Holy Spirit). Just as the qualities of those whom Paul mentioned were diverse, so it is within the church. Everyone has some part to play. Talents and gifts may vary, but the purpose is the same: to work as a team for God's glory. Ask God to show you your role if you don't already know it. Your church needs you.

Postscript

Maybe you have been reading this book and you are not a Christian. Perhaps you have been wondering how you can come into a personal relationship with Jesus Christ. Here are some pointers that may lead you to that place of blessing.

Realise that you are a sinner before a Holy God (*Romans 3:23*).

Recognise that sin separates us from God forever (*Romans 6:23*).

Repent of your sin (*2nd Peter 3:9*).

Recall how Jesus loved you so much that He died on the cross for your sins (*John 3:16*).

Request for Jesus to save you. Call on His Name (*Romans 10:13*).

Receive His free gift of salvation through faith (*John 1:12*).

Assurance of salvation comes through believing what God has said. Simply take Him at His Word (*1st John 5:13*).

Read and pray regularly to learn more about Jesus and come closer to Him each day (*Psalm 119:105, Philippians 4:6*).

Find a church that preaches the good news of salvation and fellowship regularly with other believers (*Hebrews 10:25*).

Seek the Baptism of the Holy Spirit for power to serve God. Witness to others and tell them about Jesus (*Matthew 3:11, 28:19*).

Make a public declaration of your faith in Jesus by being baptized in water. This does not save you, but comes after salvation. It is an act of obedience and a declaration of faith (*Acts 2:41*).

Perhaps you have been saved for a number of years but are not in that place that you know you should be. I would ask you to take a look in your 'mind's eye' to Jesus on that cross and remember what He did for you there. Remember His love for you. Come back to Jesus today and don't put it off any longer (*Luke 15:20*).

Jesus is coming again. Watch and be ready.

BVPRI - #0002 - 111122 - C0 - 229/152/9 - PB - 9781739201807 - Gloss Lamination